GOD WAS INCARNATE AND BECAME MAN

METROPOLITAN YOUSSEF

Edited and translated by
St. Mary and St. Moses Abbey

ST MARY & MOSES ABBEY PRESS

God was Incarnate and Became Man
By Metropolitan Youssef

Copyright © 2025 Coptic Orthodox Diocese of the Southern U.S.A.

Designed & Published by:
St. Mary & St. Moses Abbey Press
101 S Vista Dr, Sandia, TX 78383
stmabbeypress.com

Cover icon was written by the iconographer Gergis Samir.

All Scripture quotations in the footnotes of this book, unless otherwise
indicated, are taken from the New King James Version® Copyright © 1982 by
Thomas Nelson, Inc. Used by permission. All rights reserved.

The following Septuagint text is used when indicated: *The Septuagint Version of
the Old Testament*. (London, UK: Samuel Bagster and Sons, 1879).

Contents

✠

God the Father begot God the Son without time, and made Him of a Virgin in time. The first nativity exceeds times; the second nativity enlightens times. Yet both nativities are marvelous; the one without a mother, the other without a father. When God begot the Son, He begot Him of Himself, not of a mother; when the Mother gave birth to her Son, she gave Him birth as a Virgin, not by man. He was born of the Father without a beginning; He was born of a mother, as to-day at an appointed beginning. Born of the Father He made us; born of a mother He re-made us. He was born of the Father, that we might be; He was born of a mother, that we might not be lost.

St. Augustine of Hippo

Sermon XC 2. (NPNF[1] 6)

Introduction

The Story Behind the Feast of Nativity

For approximately three centuries, the Church did not celebrate the Feast of Nativity. That is why we do not know when exactly Jesus was born, and some scholars say that most probably He was born around March or September. Why? Because the shepherds would not be outside all night long in the very cold weather in December, or in the very hot weather in June or July. So most probably this happened during March or September. But why do we celebrate it in December or January? And by the way, we can say that all of us celebrate on December 25th: the West celebrates it on December 25th according to the Gregorian calendar, but we celebrate it on December 25th according to the Julian calendar, because according to the Julian calendar, December 25th corresponds to January 7th. Technically, we are not celebrating on January 7th but on December 25th, because there is a 13-day difference between the two calendars.

Why did we choose December 25th? There was a Pagan feast called the feast of the sun. What is the feast of the sun? The hours of the day start to shorten until December, and then around December 21st, the days start to be longer a little bit, and then the days become longer and longer until June 21st. And after June 21st the days start to be short again. So, according to Paganism, when the days start to be longer, they celebrate a feast called the feast of the sun because now the day becomes longer, which means the sun will stay longer on the feast.

When Christianity replaced Paganism, the fathers of the church wanted the people to completely forget about Paganism, so they replaced the Pagan feast with the Christian feast. So they said that Jesus indeed is the Light who came to the world, as we read in the first chapter of the Gospel of St. John. Jesus is the Sun of righteousness, as we read in the book of Malachi.[1] Therefore, they said that we celebrate the birth of our Lord Jesus Christ when the day starts to be longer, and they chose December 25th to be the Feast of Nativity, replacing the Pagan feast of the sun with this Christian feast, the birth of our Lord Jesus Christ. So December 25th is not the historical day of the birth of our Lord Jesus Christ. We do not know when the Lord Jesus was born. And to eliminate confusion, all of us are celebrating on December 25th, but according to either the Julian calendar or the Gregorian calendar, there being a 13-day difference between the two calendars.

---

1   See Malachi 4:2.

But in every respect, too, He is man, the formation of God; and thus He took up man into Himself, the invisible becoming visible, the incomprehensible being made comprehensible, the impassible becoming capable of suffering, and the Word being made man, thus summing up all things in Himself : so that as in super-celestial, spiritual, and invisible things, the Word of God is supreme, so also in things visible and corporeal He might possess the supremacy, and, taking to Himself the pre-eminence, as well as constituting Himself Head of the Church, He might draw all things to Himself at the proper time.

St. Irenaeus

Against Heresies III.XVI.6 (ANF 1)

1

The Genealogy of the Lord Jesus Christ

Society in Biblical times was organized along family and tribal lines. Genealogy was of importance in establishing a person's lineage. Religious importance was determined by who your forefathers were. For example, only the descendants of Aaron could become priests.[2] Temple officials had to examine extensively the genealogy of those presented for the priesthood. Old Testament genealogies also reminded the Israelites of their history as the chosen people of God. Genealogies in the Holy Scripture are not meant to be an exact, detailed lineage of birth, nor are they always complete. For example, the list of Aaron's descendants in the first book of Chronicles (6:3–15) includes names that do not appear in Aaron's genealogy in the

---

2   See Exodus 28:1.

Book of Ezra.[3] Genealogies are thought to primarily establish a family's link with the past.

"And Adam lived one hundred and thirty years, and begot a son in his own likeness, after his image, and named him Seth."[4]

There are only two genealogies in the New Testament. The Gospels of St. Matthew and St. Luke trace the ancestry of the Lord Jesus Christ back to Abraham and Adam, respectively. Though both genealogies are not exactly alike, the ancestries were included in the Gospels to emphasize that the Lord Jesus was a son of King David, which was the necessary lineage for the Messiah.

Both of the Gospels show the distinction of the birth of the newborn Lord Jesus. St. Matthew in his gospel emphasizes the Lord Jesus' royal lineage, listing kings in the house of David among his ancestors and telling of a miraculous star that proclaimed the coming of a new "King of the Jews."[5] St. Matthew also introduced "wise men from the East"[6] who recognized the significance of the star's meaning and brought unto the Newborn Lord gifts of gold, frankincense, and myrrh.

The message of the Gospel of St. Matthew is very straightforward. The Lord Jesus Christ is the promised Messiah of biblical prophecy. The Lord Jesus Christ

---

3   See Ezra 7:1–5.

4   Genesis 5:3.

5   Matthew 2:2.

6   Matthew 2:1.

was born with the purpose of leading all humanity toward salvation.

St. Luke emphasized the humility of the newborn Lord Jesus Christ. The newborn Lord was born within lowly surroundings, a cave in the hills around Bethlehem, where domestic animals were kept at night. This is where His divinity was manifested. The infant Lord Jesus' first bed was in a feeding trough for animals. His holy birth was announced neither to kings nor priests but to shepherds in the field. This is truly the Lamb of God and the true Shepherd born to lead His people.

In the Gospel of St. Luke, we can understand the people and events that occurred during the time of the birth and early life of the Lord. It is through the humanitarian aspects of the Gospel of St. Luke that we see the Lord Jesus Christ's concern for sinners and the outcast, the poor, the sick, and women. St. Luke further traces the ancestry of the Lord Jesus Christ through the non-royal descendants of King David.

Then the angel said to them, "Do not be afraid, for behold, I bring you good tidings of great joy which will be to all people. For there is born to you this day in the city of David a Savior, who is Christ the Lord. And this will be the sign to you: You will find a Babe wrapped in swaddling cloths, lying in a manger." And suddenly there was with the angel a multitude of the heavenly host praising God and saying: "Glory to God in the highest, And on earth peace, goodwill toward men!"[7]

The Gospel of St. Luke is unique in its depiction of the Lord's birth. Perhaps this can be attributed to the growing lack of faith in the Christian communities, resulting from their belief that the promised return of the Messiah had been delayed. Writing in southern Greece primarily for Gentile converts to Christianity, St. Luke emphasizes the universal significance of the Holy Gospel for all mankind, not only for the Jews.

Further, the other Gospels called upon the immediacy of the Kingdom of God, while St. Luke writes of the Lord Jesus Christ beginning His holy ministry not by announcing the imminent coming of the kingdom of heaven but by the presence of the Holy Spirit working through Him.[8]

St. Luke showed the humility of the Lord Jesus Christ in a manner considered worthy of the One born to redeem mankind. St. Luke details the Lord Jesus Christ's concern and love for sinners with the confident hope of their repentance and forgiveness.

Both Gospels described how a virgin, St. Mary, betrothed to St. Joseph, mysteriously conceived the Lord Jesus Christ. They further detail how the holy Infant was born in Bethlehem as a descendant of King David. Both

---

7   Luke 2:10–14.

8   See Luke 4:14.

gospel writers also show the newborn Lord as the eternal Son of God. Further, it is definitely emphasized that all this occurred in fulfillment of the ancient prophecies.

Although many often think of the town of Bethlehem as small, it is definitely not insignificant. Bethlehem is known as the burial place of Jacob's wife Rachel, the birthplace of King David, and above all, the birthplace of the Messiah.

The genealogies differ in that St. Matthew derives the Davidic ancestry through King Solomon, son of David, while St. Luke traces the Davidic descent through another son of David, Nathan. St. Luke's genealogy goes beyond Abraham, the father of all nations, to Adam to emphasize the Lord's unity with the entire human race.[9]

St. Luke describes St. Joseph as the son of Heli.[10] St. Matthew states that Jacob begot Joseph.[11] Is there a conflict in the Gospel writing here?

In the Book of Deuteronomy (25:5–6), there is mention of a law that states that the brother of a man who died without a child should marry the wife of the deceased and raise an heir for his brother. The most probable explanation for these two verses is that Jacob and Heli were born of the same mother, but to two different fathers. When Heli died following a barren marriage, his brother Jacob married the widow he left behind, who then became the mother of St. Joseph.

9   See Luke 3:38.

10   See Luke 3:23.

11   See Matthew 1:16.

The Gospels were not meant to provide a detailed description of the Lord Jesus Christ. The Gospels do not describe His appearance, tell of His education, nor of His psychological development. The Gospels are meant to portray Him as an icon does a saint. We identify with the Lord Jesus Christ through His sayings and teachings. The Gospels of St. Matthew and St. Luke tell us all that we need to know of the early life of the Lord Jesus Christ.

No matter how wise or smart we may think we are, no matter how much knowledge we acquire, or how experienced we become, we will never be able to fully understand everything about heaven, mankind, or the universe in which we live. God has hidden the great mysteries of His wisdom from all of us, particularly those of us who believe ourselves to be wise and educated. Instead, only He can choose to whom He will reveal the truths of biblical life, how we should live, and how to gain wisdom.

> *Immaculate and undefiled was His generation: for where the Holy Spirit breathes, there all pollution is taken away: undefiled from the Virgin was the incarnate generation of the Only-begotten.*

> ### St. Cyril of Jerusalem
>
> *Lecture XII* 32. (NPNF[2] 7)

2

The Prophecy of Zacharias

Enlightening Our Lives

Zacharias, in his prophecy, explained why God is visiting us, why God is seeking us, why God is searching for us, and why He decided to be incarnate and to become man. He said, "Through the tender mercy of our God, with which the Dayspring from on high has visited us."[12] So this tender mercy, this love, this compassion in the Holy Trinity made the Son of God become incarnate and visit us. So He did not do it out of obligation or out of necessity or out of routine or duty; He did it out of love. Through the tender mercy of our God the Father with which the Dayspring, the Son, who is shining on us from on high, has visited us. So the incarnation was the will and the pleasure of the Holy Trinity. By the will of the Son, the approval of the Father, and the pleasure of the

---

12 Luke 1:78.

Holy Spirit, the incarnation was fulfilled, and God has visited us here on earth.

But what is the purpose of this visitation? Many things. Before the incarnation of the Son of God as we read in Isaiah, "The people who walked in darkness have seen a great light; those who dwelt in the land of the shadow of death, upon them a light has shined,"[13] and we hear in every Divine Liturgy according to St. Basil, "[We] were sitting in darkness and the shadow of death."[14] Once we separated ourselves from God, we began living in darkness and became blind because God is light. So when we separate ourselves from the true Light, we are in darkness. But when the Dayspring shone from on high upon us, He enlightened our lives, as Zacharias said, "To give light to those who sit in darkness and the shadow of death."[15] He enlightened our way by His knowledge. He opened our internal eye, not only to see Him, but to be united in Him and be one with Him. So, He came to enlighten our lives after we were sitting in darkness.

We were sitting in the shadow of death. The shadow of death means that we were on the verge of death, we were under the sentence of death. Therefore, if He had not become incarnate, if He had not visited us, we would have been executed, would have been thrown into the lake of fire for eternity, all of us with no exception.

---

13   Isaiah 9:2.

14   The Divine Liturgy of St. Basil – Holy.

15   Luke 1:79.

Guiding our Feet into the Way of Peace

Another reason is to guide our feet into the way of peace. Can you imagine if a person is sitting in darkness or is blind, and this person is waiting to be killed? This person will definitely have no peace. But when God came, and enlightened our lives, and delivered us from death to life, and dropped all the charges against us, we now know the way of peace. Peace with God after the enmity for almost 5500 years. There was enmity between heaven and earth, between God and us. Now, through the cross of the Lord Jesus Christ, we are reconciled with the Father; we are reconciled with heaven once again. Also, there is peace between the person and his brother. Jews and Gentiles were enemies, but through the incarnation of the Son of God, the two became one. The Gentiles and Jews became one, and also peace between the person and himself. So God came to bring peace, to guide our feet into the way of peace. That is why in the incarnation of the Son of God, the angels praised and said, "Glory to God in the highest, and on earth peace, goodwill toward men!"[16]

A Permanent Horn of Salvation

As Zacharias said, "Blessed is the Lord God of Israel, for He has visited and redeemed His people."[17] Redemption

---

16   Luke 2:14.

17   Luke 1:68.

means that you need to sacrifice something to redeem something else; that is the concept of redemption. So, who is sacrificed here? It is God, the Lord Jesus Christ. He offered Himself as a sacrifice, as a sin sacrifice, as a trespass sacrifice, as a peace offering, and as a burnt offering. All these sacrifices in the Old Testament were fulfilled in the person of our Lord Jesus Christ. He came in order to redeem us. He offered Himself as a ransom, a ransom for all of us. He paid for our sins in order to redeem us from the sentence of death. And not only did He redeem us, but as Zacharias said also in his prophecy, "[He] has raised up a horn of salvation for us in the house of His servant David."[18]

What does "a horn of salvation" mean? God visited us to be the horn of our salvation. In the Old Testament, in the tabernacle of meeting, the altar had four horns, and if anyone, for example, killed somebody by mistake, not intentionally, in order not to be killed, he used to run to the temple and hold the horn of the altar; once he holds the horn of the altar, nobody can kill him. So, Zacharias has this image, and he imagined that the Lord Jesus Christ came to be the horn of our salvation. When we hold onto Him, when we cling to Him, nobody can hurt us; we will not die. We will not be under the sentence of death if we are holding onto the horn of our salvation.

How can we die if we are holding onto the source of life and the fountain of life? That is why the Lord

---

18   Luke 1:69.

said, "Those who are in My hand nobody can touch them, nobody can hurt them."[19] So this visitation, God has visited us not only to enlighten our life, not only to move us from death to life, not only to guide us into the way of peace, not only to redeem us, but also to be a permanent horn of salvation. Every time we run to Him and hold onto Him, then again nobody can touch us, nobody can harm us, nobody can kill us. We have this horn of salvation every day on the altar. When we come and partake of His Body and His Blood as the Lord said, "Whoever eats My flesh and drinks My blood has eternal life, and I will raise him up at the last day."[20]

Salvation from our Enemies

The purpose of this visitation is also "that we should be saved from our enemies and from the hand of all who hate us."[21] We have many enemies. Satan is the biggest enemy to all of us. But there are many enemies with the fall of Adam and Eve. Illness and diseases became enemies. Death became another enemy as St. Paul said, "The last enemy that will be destroyed is death."[22] Corruption is another enemy. Evil is another enemy. The bad desires of the flesh are another enemy. The world and the temptation of the world are another enemy.

---

19 Cf. John 10:28.

20 John 6:54.

21 Luke 1:71.

22 1 Corinthians 15:26.

But when Jesus came, Jesus came to give us salvation from all our enemies and from the hand of all who hate us. Now all these enemies can be defeated. As the Lord said, "In the world you will have tribulation; but be of good cheer, I have overcome the world."[23] He came and went through all these temptations, and He resembled us in everything except for sin alone to give us this victory and to give us this salvation from all our enemies and from all who hate us.

He was born—but He had been begotten: He was born of a woman—but she was a Virgin. The first is human, the second Divine. In His Human nature He had no Father, but also in His Divine Nature no Mother. Both these belong to Godhead. He dwelt in the womb—but He was recognized by the Prophet, himself still in the womb, leaping before the Word, for Whose sake He came into being.

Gregory of Nazianzus

The Third Theological Oration XIX. (NPNF[2] 7)

---

23   John 16:33.

3

Why was the Son of God Incarnate? Part One

He Came to be a Servant to the Circumcision

In the epistle of St. Paul to the Romans (15:8–9), St. Paul said, "Now I say that Jesus Christ has become a servant to the circumcision for the truth of God, to confirm the promises made to the fathers, and that the Gentiles might glorify God for His mercy, as it is written: 'For this reason I will confess to You among the Gentiles and sing to Your name.'"

St. Paul is saying that Jesus Christ came to our world to be a servant to the circumcision. What does it mean to be a servant to the circumcision? Circumcision here refers to the Jewish nation, the Jewish people. Before Christ, they used to classify the world into Jews and Gentiles. And the sign or the mark of the covenant between the Jews and God was the circumcision. So they classified the world as either circumcised or uncircumcised. So the Lord was born as a Jew. He came from a Jewish family. His ancestors are Jewish. Yes, He was born of St. Mary without the seed of man, but St. Mary was also of Jewish origin. And He came to serve His nation, the Jews. This is what he meant by saying, "Servant to the circumcision."

But what kind of service? How would He serve the Jews? We will find the answer in the Gospel of St. Mark when the Lord said, "The Son of Man did not come to be served, but to serve, and to give His life a ransom for many."[24] So the service that the Lord did to the Jews was that He offered Himself as a ransom on their behalf. He came to die. He came to be a sacrifice. And that is the reason why He was born among the animals. The main reason He was born among the animals is because He is the Lamb of God. He came to offer Himself; He is our Passover Lamb. So when St. Paul said He became a servant to the circumcision, he meant that He came to offer Himself as a sacrifice, and thus, He is serving His people who believed in Him, who accepted Him.

He Came to Confirm the Promises Made to the Fathers

St. Paul said, "For the truth of God…"[25] What does "for the truth of God" mean? To prove that God is

24   Mark 10:45.

25   Romans 15:8.

true, to validate the truth and the faithfulness of God. So, He was incarnate and became man to establish and reveal to all of us that God is true.

I would like to reflect on validating the truth of God, and why it is important for us that the Lord Jesus Christ validate to us and establish to us the truth and the faithfulness of God the Father. It is clear that St. Paul made a distinction between Christ confirming the truth of God and Christ confirming the promises made to the fathers. At first glance, we might say he is saying the same thing, for we say that He is confirming the truth of God because He confirms the promises made to the fathers. But there is a big difference between confirming the truth of God and confirming the promises to the fathers. What does confirming the truth of God mean? It means that God is true even before He makes any promises.

God is true because He is the definition of truth. As He said, "I am the truth."[26] If we said that God is only true because His promises are true, then this means that God is only true in relation to us, as if this attribute of God, that He is true, has no meaning unless we exist; He has to make promises to us in order to be true. But St. Paul is saying, "No. God is self-sufficient. He is true by Himself because He is the definition of truth." For us, when I say, "This person is faithful," I need to measure him against a standard to say that this person is faithful. But for God, there is no standard,

---

26   John 14:6.

because He is the standard: "I am the truth." Therefore, God cannot measure Himself against something else because He is the definition of the truth.

And we can say that all things are true to the degree that they conform to who God is and what He says. When we say this principle is true, or this person is faithful, how do we define it? How do we say that this is a true teacher or that is a false prophet, this is a true religion or that is a false religion? What is the standard here? It is God. So anything is true in relation to, or to the degree that they conform to who God is and what He says. That is why St. Paul made a distinction between His promises and to validate that God is true in Himself. St. Paul says to St. Timothy, "If we deny Him, He will deny us, but if we are faithless, He remains faithful; He cannot deny Himself."[27] What does it mean that He cannot deny Himself? It means He cannot be untrue to Himself, because He is the definition of the truth.

But how is this relevant to me? How is it relevant to me that God is true and that He is committed to His truth, to Himself? If God is not a true God in Himself, then actually everything would be false. There is no true God. There is no eternal life. There is no everlasting joy. Then, everything will fall apart. As St. Paul said, "If Christ is not risen, your faith is futile."[28] So Christ came to show us and to demonstrate

---

27 2 Timothy 2:12–13.
28 1 Corinthians 15:17.

to us that God is true in Himself. So when we abide in Him, we abide in the truth. When we believe in Him, we believe in unchanging truth, in absolute truth that can never be changed, and this gives us stability in our lives.

If everything is false and relative, then actually, we will be living in a world of chaos. But God is true. The second point that St. Paul is making: And because He is true, it is imperative that His promises be true. If God is true, then His promises are true. That is why he said, "Jesus Christ has become a servant to the circumcision for the truth of God, to confirm the promises made to the fathers."[29] God made a promise to Adam and Eve 5,000 years before the incarnation of Jesus Christ, but in the fullness of time, He fulfilled this promise.

Many of us say, "Yes, we know that God is true and His promises are true, but we don't deserve His promises." That is why we doubt whether God would save us or not. We have doubts about His promises when He told us, "All things work together for good to those who love God."[30] But we say, "But I'm bad. I'm a sinner. Maybe if I'm a saint, then the promises are true." When the Lord said, "Do not fear, little flock, for it is your Father's good pleasure to give you the kingdom,"[31] we might say, "Yes, if I am a good person." But St. Paul is saying that when God made

29   Romans 15:8.

30   Romans 8:28.

31   Luke 12:32.

these promises, He made these promises to fallen people. He made promises to Adam and Eve, even before the repentance.

And when He came, He did not fulfill the punishment, but He fulfilled the promises of salvation. He took our punishment. That is why He came to serve us by becoming a ransom, becoming a sacrifice. He took our punishment to save us. And here we need to understand that His promises are true, not because we are worthy, but because He is good and the lover of mankind. His promises are true, and God will fulfill His promises to us, not because we are worthy. If God were dealing with us according to our worthiness, nobody would be saved. But He is dealing with us according to His goodness as the lover of mankind.

That is why He became a curse for us, as St. Paul said in the epistle to the Galatians, "Christ has redeemed us from the curse of the law, having become a curse for us."[32] That is why He died on the cross. So when I know that the promises of God are true because of who He is, not because of our worthiness, this will make us grateful to Him, and we know that everything should be through Him. That is why we conclude our prayer by saying, "in Christ Jesus our Lord," or we conclude the Thanksgiving Prayer by saying, "Through the grace, compassion, and love of mankind of Your only begotten Son." Because we

---

32   Galatians 3:13.

know if we make any request or any prayer in our name, it will not be answered, because we are not worthy. But only in the name of the Lord Jesus Christ, they will be answered, because His promises are true and His promises are based on His faithfulness, on His goodness, because He is the lover of mankind.

St. Paul, however, added something very interesting: that His promises are not promises of punishment or retaliation, but His promises are promises of mercy. He said, "That the Gentiles might glorify God for His mercy."[33] His promises are promises of mercy. And again, why did God become man? Why did He empty Himself? Why did He take the form of a man? In order to show His mercy to us. Why did He forgive our sins? Because He is merciful, because of the abundance of His mercy.

That is why when we remember the Last Day at the Judgment, we say, "According to Your mercy, O Lord, and not according to our sins." Micah the prophet exalts the mercies of God by saying, "Who is a God like You, pardoning iniquity and passing over the transgression of the remnant of His heritage? He does not retain His anger forever, because He delights in mercy."[34] God delights in showing us His mercy. And this is the meaning of the song of the angels, "Glory to God in the highest, and on earth peace, goodwill toward men!"[35] What is the goodwill toward us? To show us His mercy.

33   Romans 15:9.
34   Micah 7:18.
35   Luke 2:14.

Why? Because He delights in showing compassion and mercy upon us. St. Paul, therefore, is saying that Christ came to reveal to us that God is true, to tell us that His promises are also true, and His promises are based on His goodness, not on our worthiness, and also that His promises are promises of mercy.

> *Understand, man, the depth of the mystery! God was in visible form like unto us: the Lord of all in the likeness of a slave, albeit the glory of lordship is inseparable from Him. Understand that the Only-begotten was made flesh; that He endured to be born of a woman for our sakes, to put away the curse pronounced upon the first woman.*[36]

St. Cyril of Alexandria

He Came to Save Us

The Lord Jesus Christ will not only be a servant to the circumcision, but the salvation of the Lord will expand to include the Gentiles also. As we read in the epistle to the Romans, "And that the Gentiles might glorify God for His mercy, as it is written: 'For this reason I will confess to You among the Gentiles, and

---

36 St. Cyril of Alexandria, *A Commentary upon the Gospel according to S. Luke*, Smith R.P., trans. (Oxford University Press, 1859), 13.

sing to Your name.'"[37] St. Paul is basically saying that God became man to serve us, to be a servant to the circumcision and a servant to the Gentiles, to the Jews and the Gentiles. And what kind of service? To offer Himself as a ransom, to die, to be our Passover Lamb.

When Adam and Eve sinned, there was a punishment, which was death. As St. Paul the Apostle says, "Therefore, just as through one man sin entered the world, and death through sin, and thus death spread to all men, because all sinned."[38] Therefore, we sinned in Adam. And as sin entered the world through one man, so did death enter the whole world. In the Coptic text of the verse, there is an extra word after "all sinned," which is translated to "in him,"[39] meaning that we all sinned in Adam. We were all in Adam, and when Adam sinned, we all sinned. Therefore, we were all under the sentence of death. When our Lord Jesus Christ came, and took our humanity, and died on the cross, and fulfilled the sentence of death, now whoever believes in Christ and unites with Him has died with Christ and risen with Him, and is a new creation. We die with Christ in Baptism: "Buried with Him in baptism,"[40] that is, the person who was born of a father and mother dies. And when we rise from the baptismal water, we are born of the Spirit: "That which is born of the flesh is flesh, and that which is born of the Spirit is

---

37   Romans 15:9.

38   Romans 5:12.

39   Ⲫⲛⲉⲧⲁⲩⲉⲣⲛⲟⲃⲓ ⲛ̀ϧⲏⲧϥ [all sinned in him].

40   Colossians 2:12.

spirit."[41] We are a new creation.[42] Therefore, salvation is one of the reasons for the incarnation.

He Came to Defeat Sin

Our Lord Jesus Christ took a complete human body, a complete human nature, and He lived His life on earth without committing any sin, as we say in the Divine Liturgy, "You, without change, were incarnate and became man and resembled us in everything, except for sin alone."[43] Here God gave this body and this human nature the ability to triumph over sin and to live without falling into sin if perfect union with God takes place. As St. John said, "Whoever is born of God does not sin,"[44] because the Son of God did not sin. Therefore, if I unite with God, I also receive this ability, the victory over sin. But because of our weakness, and our inclination, and our free will, we turn back and sin. God, however, out of His love, gave us the Mystery of Repentance and Confession, and of Communion, so that "if anyone sins, we have an Advocate with the Father, Jesus Christ the righteous,"[45] as St. John said. Through the Mysteries, sins are forgiven: "The blood of Jesus Christ His Son cleanses us from all sin."[46]

---

41 John 3:6.

42 See 2 Corinthians 5:17.

43 The Divine Liturgy of St. Gregory – Prayer of Reconciliation.

44 1 John 5:18.

45 1 John 2:1.

46 1 John 1:7.

He Came to Defeat Death

God is immortal, and if God had not allowed death to come near Him, He would not have died in His incarnation. Our Lord, however, allowed death to come near Him. All of us, our life ends with death, whether because of illness or old age. But the Lord said, "I have power to lay it down, and I have power to take it again."[47] "Lay it down," that is, death; "take it," that is, resurrection. Therefore, we say a precise expression in the Divine Liturgy of St. Cyril: "the death, which He accepted by His own will for us all."[48] And in the Divine Liturgy of St. Gregory, we say, "For in the same night in which You gave Yourself up of Your own will and authority alone."[49] God's will and authority determined the moment of death. "His own will" means His perfect will. Therefore, when Pilate said to Jesus, "'Do You not know that I have power to crucify You, and power to release You?' Jesus answered, 'You could have no power at all against Me unless it had been given you from above.'"[50] "I have power to lay it down, and I have power to take it again."[51] Why did He accept death in human nature? To defeat death by His resurrection. In the Hymn of the Resurrection, we say, "Christ is risen from the dead, trampling down death by death and upon those in the tombs bestowing eternal life." Therefore,

---

47 John 10:18.
48 Institution Narrative.
49 Institution Narrative.
50 John 19:10–11.
51 John 10:18.

when we die, we will rise again. How? Through the resurrection of Christ. Because God defeated death in human nature, now human nature has the ability to rise and be immortal with God. "And upon those in the tombs bestowing eternal life."

He Came to Remove Corruption from the World

We all know the story of the fall of Adam and Eve, and the sin, transgression, disobedience, and corruption that humanity suffered after the fall. As we say in the Prayer of Reconciliation in the Divine Liturgy, "O God, the Great, the Eternal, who formed man in incorruption." Through the fall, however, corruption entered the world and sin entered the world, as St. Paul said, "Through one man sin entered the world, and death through sin, and thus death spread to all men."[52]

The entire human nature was corrupted because of sin. Therefore, God was incarnate to treat this human nature, which was corrupted. In the Thursday Theotokia, we say to the Virgin Mary, "She gave all the form of humanity, completely, to God, the Creator and the Word of the Father." Our Lord took our nature completely: body, soul, and spirit. This is to free human nature from corruption. When I unite to Christ in the water of Baptism, my nature is freed from corruption also. We are born sinners and with a

---

52   Romans 5:12.

corrupted nature. When a person is immersed in the water of Baptism, the old corrupted man dies in the water and is buried, then he rises as a new creation. If I sin, my human nature is renewed by Repentance, Confession, and Communion. This new nature is symbolized by the white garments, as is said in the Book of Revelation: "These are the ones who come out of the great tribulation, and washed their robes and made them white in the blood of the Lamb."[53]

This sin that is directed against God, how is it remitted? This death that has spread to all, who can destroy it? Who can defeat it? And this corruption that entered all humanity, who can remove it from humanity? No one on earth can destroy the power of death, nor can any remove corruption from humanity; why? Because "they have all turned aside; they have together become unprofitable; there is none who does good, no, not one."[54] Therefore, if all have turned aside and become corrupt—that is, corruption has entered all—how can a human being, into whom corruption has entered, save others? There is, then, no human being on earth who can save others.

How about the angels and archangels? Can they save? First of all, the angels are limited; therefore, how can a limited angel redeem the unlimited world? Who can atone for all the sins of all people in all ages? Also, the Scripture says about God that "He charges His

---

53   Revelation 7:14.

54   Romans 3:12.

angels with error."[55] So, how can an angel save man? And as we say in the Divine Liturgy according to St. Gregory, "Neither an angel nor an archangel, neither a patriarch nor a prophet, have You entrusted with our salvation." From here, it became necessary that God be incarnate; God was incarnate so that He may unite to our humanity. And when the All-holy God unites to our humanity, into which corruption has entered, our Lord removes this corruption from the world.

God was incarnate because He loves us, and love compelled our Lord to be incarnate, as we say in the Holy Psalmody, "He was overcome by His compassion,"[56] meaning that the love of our Lord overcame Him and made Him become incarnate and become man for our sakes. Is it conceivable that the Lord sees the creation that He created perish, and He does not rescue it? It is impossible.

Therefore, the incarnation is the story of God's love for humanity. This is the same story that the Lord declared to Moses the prophet in the past, for the bush is one of the symbols of the incarnation. The Lord saw the people of Israel oppressed in the land of Egypt, and Egyptian taskmasters made their burden heavier. The people cried out to God from the oppression, "so God heard their groaning."[57] What next? The Lord heard, so what would He do? Moses was once walking in the mountain and saw a bush, and the bush was

---

55   Job 4:18.

56   Monday Theotokia, Part 5.

57   Exodus 2:24.

burning with fire but was not consumed. The scene was strange, of course. So Moses said, "I will now turn aside and see this great sight."[58] How is it that this bush is burning with fire but is not consumed?

As soon as Moses drew near, the Lord said to him, "Do not draw near this place. Take your sandals off your feet, for the place where you stand is holy ground."[59] And indeed Moses took his sandals off, and then the Lord began to talk with him. He said to him, "I am the God of your father—the God of Abraham, the God of Isaac, and the God of Jacob."[60] But, Lord, what is the story of this bush that is burning with fire? The Lord said to him, "I have surely seen the oppression of My people who are in Egypt, and have heard their cry because of their taskmasters, for I know their sorrows. So I have come down to deliver them."[61] He saw and heard, and then He came down to deliver them: that is, the incarnation. The Lord began to prepare humanity, that God, our God, is a consuming fire. Our God, this divinity, the fire comes down to our humanity, to our world, and unites with our humanity, and the fire does not burn the body, as the fire did not burn the bush. The thought of the incarnation: the Lord came down so that He might save humanity.

---

58   Exodus 3:3.
59   Exodus 3:5.
60   Exodus 3:6.
61   Exodus 3:7–8.

It was opportunely, then, that the Savior shone upon us in our great tribulation when he was born of a woman in regard to the flesh, that he might save man born of a woman, and, having loosed him from the bonds of death, might teach him to say joyfully, "O death, where is your victory? Hell, where is your sting?"[62]

St. Cyril of Alexandria

---

62 St. Cyril of Alexandria, *Festal Letters 1–12*, Amidon P.R., trans.; O'Keefe J.J., ed. (Washington, DC: The Catholic University of America Press, 2009), 39.

4

Why was the Son of God Incarnate? Part Two

He Came to Reveal to us the Knowledge of God

Another reason for the incarnation is that the Lord Jesus Christ came to reveal to us the knowledge of God. "No one has seen God at any time. The only begotten Son, who is in the bosom of the Father, He has declared Him."[63] We did not know God. We were ignorant of the knowledge of God. But the Son revealed God the Father to us. This is why theology is not by speculation or by making hypotheses, and then you try to prove it. Theology is by revelation, and this revelation is through the only begotten Son.

---

63   John 1:18.

He Came to Reconcile us to God the Father

Another reason for the incarnation of the Son of God is that He reconciled us to God the Father. After the fall of Adam and Eve, there was enmity between us and God. But when God sent His Son to the world, He reconciled the people together through the cross. He reconciled the Jews with the Gentiles in His body, and then He reconciled both of them to God the Father. As St. Paul explained in his epistle to the Ephesians, how the Lord Jesus Christ on the cross reconciled the Jews with the Gentiles.[64] Then, He reconciled both of them to God the Father. And through this reconciliation, we inherited the kingdom of God. We inherited eternal life because we are one with the Son, and the Son is the only heir of eternal life, as St. Paul said in the epistle to the Hebrews, "His Son, whom He has appointed heir of all things."[65] Therefore, in the Son we also became heirs of eternal life.

He Came to Restore the Love and Oneness Between One Another

Whoever is living the true incarnation must have love for others. In the Gospel of St. John, the Scripture says, "He would gather together in one the children of God who were scattered abroad."[66] This is one of the reasons for the incarnation, that God may gather

---

64   See Ephesians 2:16.

65   Hebrews 1:2.

66   John 11:52.

us together in one. He says, "And there will be one flock and one shepherd."[67] Through the Mysteries of the Church, we become one. For example, through Baptism, we become one: "For by one Spirit we were all baptized into one body—whether Jews or Greeks, whether slaves or free—and have all been made to drink into one Spirit [which is in Myron]."[68] We are one in Communion also, for St. Paul says, "For we, though many, are one bread and one body; for we all partake of that one bread."[69] For this reason, we use one bread—one Corban—for all of us to partake of. St. Paul also says, "For as many of you as were baptized into Christ have put on Christ. There is neither Jew nor Greek, there is neither slave nor free, there is neither male nor female; for you are all one in Christ Jesus."[70] In the incarnation, because God took our body, and we became members in the body of Christ, we ought to live the oneness in love. The devil attacked this in the fall; therefore, we have to live it in the incarnation.

He Came to Restore the Lost Sheep

Also, our Lord Jesus Christ in His incarnation came to restore the lost sheep, as He said, "And other sheep I have which are not of this fold; them also I must bring, and they will hear My voice; and there will

---

67   John 10:16.
68   1 Corinthians 12:13. Words in brackets are added for clarity.
69   1 Corinthians 10:17.
70   Galatians 3:27–28.

be one flock and one shepherd."[71] The Gentiles in the Old Testament were lost. They were Pagan. They worshipped idols. But in His incarnation, the Lord came to restore the lost sheep, whether the lost sheep of Israel, as He said to the twelve disciples when He sent them, "Go rather to the lost sheep of the house of Israel,"[72] or the Gentiles, the Pagans who did not know God. He came to reconcile them and to restore the lost sheep into the sheepfold. He gave us the parable of the lost sheep, how the Good Shepherd left the ninety-nine to seek and to search for the lost sheep.

He Came to Unite with Humanity

In our prayers, we always speak about the Holy Trinity: the Father and the Son and the Holy Spirit. The Father is the Origin of existence. And the eternal kingdom, the kingdom of heaven, is the kingdom of the Father, as St. Paul the Apostle says in his first epistle to the Corinthians:

> For He [the Son] must reign till He has put all enemies under His feet. The last enemy that will be destroyed is death.... Now when all things are made subject to Him [to the Father], then the Son Himself will also be subject to Him who put all things under Him, that God may be all in all.[73]

---

71 John 10:16.

72 Matthew 10:6.

73 1 Corinthians 15:25–26, 28. Words in brackets are added for

What does this mean? It means that the Son is presently reigning, as we say in our prayers, "Our Lord, God, Savior, and King of us all, Jesus Christ." The reign of the Son began on the cross: "The Lord reigned on a wood."[74] Therefore, the King over us presently is God the Son, our Lord Jesus Christ. The Son reigns over us until He subdues all the enemies, and the last enemy that will be subdued is death, because death is still working. After He subdues all enemies, the Son will hand over the kingship to God the Father, that He may be all in all. This means that the eternal kingdom is the kingdom of God the Father. For this reason, in the Lord's Prayer, we say, "Your kingdom come." We are here not talking about the kingdom of the Son, for the Son has already reigned since the cross: "The Lord reigned on a wood."[75] But rather we say, "Your kingdom come"; we are talking about a kingdom that will come.

Why am I explaining this point? Because I would like to move with you to another point: that is, who is worthy of inheriting the kingdom, who has the right of inheritance? According to earthly laws, the children are the ones who inherit. The son inherits; the hireling does not. This is the same understanding that St. Paul said in his epistle to the Romans, "We are children of God, and if children, then heirs."[76] Therefore, to inherit the kingdom of heaven, we have to be children,

---

clarity.

74   Psalms 95:9, according to the Coptic text of the Psalms.

75   Ibid.

76   Romans 8:17.

because if there is no sonship—if we are not children—we cannot inherit.

The Father has one only begotten Son: "The only begotten Son, who is in the bosom of the Father, He has declared Him."[77] Therefore, this Son is the One who will inherit the kingdom. So how will we enter heaven? Through adoption. What does adoption mean? Did our Lord come and say, "I will adopt you. You are now My children"? No; in the Gospel of St. John, he says, "To them He gave the right to become children of God, to those who believe in His name."[78] Then, here, there is a right, which God gives, so that we may become His children. What does "To them He gave the right to become children of God" mean? If someone has a son, and when this son gets married, is not his wife entitled to the inheritance? Yes, she is entitled to the inheritance because, according to the law, she is called daughter-in-law. Then she is considered a daughter. She received a right to the inheritance through her marriage to the son. She became as good as a daughter, a daughter-in-law, and she is treated as the son, and she inherits.

For this reason, when the Lord Christ came into the world in His incarnation, He came as a Bridegroom to humanity. As soon as St. John the Baptist saw Him, he said, "He who has the bride is the bridegroom."[79] He said that This is the Bridegroom. He presented the Lord Christ to humanity as a Bridegroom who has come for

---

77   John 1:18.

78   John 1:12.

79   John 3:29.

betrothal. St. Paul the Apostle says the same thing, "For I have betrothed you to one husband."[80] And the Lord Christ says the same thing in the parable of the wise and foolish virgins. He likens all of us to the bride— the virgins waiting for the bridegroom. And He likened Himself to the Bridegroom. And the Book of Revelation speaks of "a bride adorned for her husband,"[81] and speaks of "the marriage supper of the Lamb."[82] There is a marriage then. And if we do a comparison study between the Gospel of St. John and the Book of Revelation, we will find that the Gospel of St. John presents Christ as a Bridegroom for humanity, while the Book of Revelation presents the Church as a bride for Christ. Then there is a marriage and communion and true, actual union between the Lord Christ the Son and the Church, the bride in this mystical marriage.

In this way, we were given the right to become the children of our Lord. How? Through our marriage to Christ, through our union with Christ, we became children of God the Father. For in marriage, it says they are no longer two but one,[83] and so Christ and the Church are not two but one. And this is what St. Paul the Apostle said, "We are children of God, and if children, then heirs—heirs of God and joint heirs with Christ."[84] Through our union with Christ, we became

---

80   2 Corinthians 11:2.

81   Revelation 21:2.

82   Revelation 19:9.

83   See Mark 10:8.

84   Romans 8:17.

heirs and became one. And this is Christ's desire, as He said, "That they also may be one in Us."[85]

Why was Christ incarnate? He was incarnate to unite with humanity, and when He unites with us, He gives us the right to be children of God, and we become heirs of the kingdom and heirs with Christ.

> *When therefore you are told that the Son of God is Son of David and of Abraham, doubt not anymore that you too, the son of Adam, shall be son of God. For not at random, nor in vain did He abase Himself so greatly, only He was minded to exalt us. Thus He was born after the flesh, that you might be born after the Spirit; He was born of a woman, that you might cease to be the son of a woman.*

St. John Chrysostom

Homilies on the Gospel of St. Matthew II.3 (NPNF[1] 10)

He Came to Make us Children of the Father

So in Christ we are children of God the Father, as St. Paul said, "He is not ashamed to call them brethren."[86] When the Lord appeared to Mary Magdalene after the resurrection, He told her, "I have not yet ascended to My Father; but go to My brethren and say to them, 'I

---

85   John 17:21.

86   Hebrews 2:11.

am ascending to My Father and your Father, and to My God and your God.'"[87] How can we understand these four terms, "My Father and your Father, My God and your God"? He is speaking about God the Father. When He said, "My Father," this is by nature because He is begotten from the Father before all ages, but when He said, "your Father," this is by adoption. We are adopted by accepting the Son and by being united with the Son. And when He said, "My God," this is through the incarnation because when He became Man, He participated with us in everything, so He is calling God the Father, "My God," through the incarnation. And "your God" is by nature because by nature God the Father is our God. So He said, "I am ascending to My Father [by nature] and your Father [by adoption], and to My God [through the incarnation] and your God [by nature]."[88]

He Came to Glorify us

Also, He came to crown us with glory and honor, as we read in the epistle to the Hebrews, "It was fitting for Him, for whom are all things and by whom are all things, in bringing many sons to glory, to make the captain of their salvation perfect through sufferings."[89] In order for us to be glorified, we need to be righteous, we need to be holy, we need to be saints. The Son

---

87 John 20:17.

88 Words in brackets are added for clarity.

89 Hebrews 2:10.

of God came and was crucified on the cross. He suffered on our behalf. So when He is glorified, we are glorified in Him and are crowned in Him. "For both He [that is, Christ] who sanctifies and those who are being sanctified are all of one [that is, of God the Father], for which reason He is not ashamed to call them brethren."[90] Jesus Christ was crowned with glory and honor, and in Him we will be crowned in glory and honor, as St. Paul said, "But we see Jesus, who was made a little lower than the angels, for the suffering of death crowned with glory and honor."[91] He suffered and died on the cross, so in this aspect, He is lower than the angels because the angels do not die. He accepted death for us, but we saw Him crowned with glory and honor to crown us with Him with glory and honor.

He Came to be Our High Priest

In the Old Testament, they used to choose the priests from among the people. This is so that they may feel for them and understand their weakness. As we read in the epistle to the Hebrews, "For every high priest taken from among men is appointed for men in things pertaining to God, that he may offer both gifts and sacrifices for sins."[92] God did not send angels to be our priests; He chose priests from among men. Why? To

90   Hebrews 2:11. Words in brackets are added for clarity.
91   Hebrews 2:9.
92   Hebrews 5:1.

have compassion on those who are ignorant and going astray because the priest is also a human being.

Jesus Christ, to be our High Priest, had to be a human being. That is why He became man. He became man to be merciful and a faithful priest. As St. Paul said, "Inasmuch then as the children have partaken of flesh and blood, He [that is, Jesus] Himself likewise shared in the same [flesh and blood], that through death He might destroy him who had the power of death, that is, the devil."[93] Then he said, "Therefore, in all things He had to be made like His brethren, that He might be a merciful and faithful High Priest in things pertaining to God, to make propitiation for the sins of the people."[94] Therefore, He had to be like us to be a merciful and faithful High Priest in things pertaining to God.

He Came to Fulfill the Obedience

Adam and Eve transgressed God's commandment by their disobedience, so He came to fulfill the obedience, and by fulfilling the obedience, He can restore us to the kingdom of God again. As we read in the epistle to the Hebrews, "Though He was a Son, yet He learned obedience by the things which He suffered."[95] And as we read in the epistle to the Philippians, "He humbled Himself and became obedient to the point of

93 Hebrews 2:14.
94 Hebrews 2:17.
95 Hebrews 5:8.

death, even the death of the cross."[96] So He fulfilled the obedience, "and having been perfected, He became the author of eternal salvation to all who obey Him."[97] He fulfilled the obedience, and when we obey Him, we will be saved. His obedience to the Father will be our obedience.

In the beginning He was, uncaused; for what is the Cause of God? But afterwards for a cause He was born. And that cause was that you might be saved, who insult Him and despise His Godhead, because of this, that He took upon Him your denser nature, having converse with Flesh by means of Mind. While His inferior Nature, the Humanity, became God, because it was united to God, and became One Person because the Higher Nature prevailed in order that I too might be made God so far as He is made Man.

St. Gregory of Nazianzus

The Third Theological Oration XIX. (NPNF[2] 7)

---

96   Philippians 2:8.

97   Hebrews 5:9.

5

Why in Bethlehem?

1. The Humility of Christ

Bethlehem was a very small city, as it is written in Micah the prophet, "But you, Bethlehem Ephrathah, though you are little among the thousands of Judah, yet out of you shall come forth to Me the One to be Ruler in Israel"[98]

So the first lesson we learn here is the humility of our Lord Jesus Christ. He was born in a very small city to teach us humility and to teach us that the real honor comes from within, not from outside, not because I live in a big city and in a luxurious house. The real honor comes from within, for who I am, not for where I live or where I was born.

---

98   Micah 5:2.

2. He is the Lamb of God

Not only was He born in a small city, but He was born in a manger in the midst of sheep and cattle. And there is a beautiful meaning for this. Why was Jesus Christ born? Jesus Christ was born to offer Himself as a sacrifice. In the epistle of St. Paul to the Hebrews, he says, "Therefore, when He [that is, Jesus] came into the world, He said [to the Father]: 'Sacrifice and offering You did not desire, but a body You have prepared for Me. In burnt offerings and sacrifices for sin You had no pleasure.'"[99]

Jesus, as the High Priest, came to offer sacrifices, but the Father said to the Son, "I have no pleasure in animal sacrifices and in offering." "But a body You have prepared for Me," which means that the Father said to the Son, "I want You to offer Yourself as a sacrifice." So here Jesus is both the High Priest and the sacrifice, as we chant in Holy Week, in the hymn called "He who offered Himself."

In the Old Testament, priests offered animals. Nobody offered himself, but Jesus offered Himself as a sacrifice: "In burnt offerings and sacrifices for sin You had no pleasure."[100] So, how did the Son respond to the Father: "Then I said, 'Behold, I have come—in the volume of the book it is written of Me—to do Your will, O God.'"[101] "For God so loved the world that

---

99 Hebrews 10:5–6. Words in brackets are added for clarity.

100 Hebrews 10:6.

101 Hebrews 10:7.

He gave His only begotten Son."[102] Therefore, the Son said to the Father, "If this is Your will for Me to offer My body as a sacrifice, then it is My pleasure." In all submission and in all obedience, He said to the Father, "This is what I will do."

This is why in the epistle to the Philippians, St. Paul said, "Let this mind be in you which was also in Christ Jesus, who, being in the form of God, did not consider it robbery to be equal with God."[103] When Jesus says, "I am God," He was not stealing this; He is indeed God, "but made Himself of no reputation, taking the form of a bondservant, and coming in the likeness of men."[104] The Coptic translation says "emptied Himself." Do you know what the difference is between bondservant and servant? A bondservant is just a politically correct word for a slave. So as if he were saying, "Taking the form a bondservant [a slave], and coming in the likeness of men. And being found in appearance as a man, He humbled Himself and became obedient to the point of death, even the death of the cross. Therefore God also has highly exalted Him and given Him the name which is above every name."[105] To what extent was He obedient to the Father? To the point of death, even the death of the cross.

Why was Jesus born in a manger among the animals? Because He is the Lamb of God. He came to

---

102 John 3:16.
103 Philippians 2:5–6.
104 Philippians 2:7.
105 Philippians 2:7–9.

offer Himself as a sacrifice. When St. John the Baptist saw Jesus, he said, "Behold! The Lamb of God who takes away the sin of the world!"[106] Therefore, it is natural—expected—that the Lamb who will carry the sins of the world, who will be slaughtered for our salvation to be born among the lambs, among the animals. This is why Jesus came and was born among the animals, to tell us, "I have come to offer Myself as a sacrifice." And what is the significance of offering Himself as a sacrifice? It is our redemption, it is our forgiveness, it is our salvation. He will die instead of all of us. He died as a ransom for our sins to grant us salvation.

God prepared the world through analogy or a story in the Old Testament. When God asked Abraham to offer his son, Abraham here represents God the Father, and Isaac represents Jesus Christ. As Abraham was willing to offer Isaac, the Father is also willing to offer His Son. Why was the Father willing to offer His Son? Because He loved us. In the epistle to the Romans, St. Paul says, "He [that is, the Father] who did not spare His own Son, but delivered Him up for us all, how shall He not with Him also freely give us all things?"[107] Children are the most precious beings to everyone. And to God the Father, the most precious being is His Son.

God loves us, and the birth of Christ declares to us how much the Father loves us. And His birth in Bethlehem declares to us that Jesus came to be a

---

106 John 1:29.

107 Romans 8:32.

sacrifice. This is how much the Father loves us. And the example of Abraham offering Isaac is a symbol of the Father giving His Son to die for our salvation. But as Isaac returns alive, because at the end He found a ram and offered this ram instead of Isaac, so Jesus also rose from the dead on the third day.

3. He is the Shepherd

Another meaning for why Jesus was born among the animals in Bethlehem is that He is also the Shepherd. In the Gospel of St. John, He said, "I am the good Shepherd."[108] His relationship with us is like a shepherd with his flocks. We hear several times in the Liturgy in "Let them exalt Him" that "He has made the fatherhood like a flock of sheep" according to Coptic and Arabic, but according to the English translation, "He has made the family like a flock of sheep." The Coptic and Arabic translations are more powerful and are more beautiful.

What does "He made fatherhood like a flock of sheep" mean? A shepherd's herd usually multiplies and increases, and grows in number. In natural fatherhood, parents used to have twelve or fifteen children, but now have one or two children. But when we read that He made fatherhood like sheep, this means that He blessed His children and added to His children every day those who were saved, as we read in the Book of Acts. So His fatherhood is different from natural

108 John 10:11.

fatherhood in that it is not limited to a certain number, but as He said to Abraham, "Blessing I will bless you, and multiplying I will multiply your descendants as the stars of the heaven and as the sand which is on the seashore."[109]

Therefore, the Lord Jesus Christ was born in Bethlehem to tell us that He is the Shepherd. He is the Shepherd who will shepherd His flock as we read in the Book of Psalms, "The LORD is my shepherd; I shall not want."[110] It is also interesting that the only people to whom the angels preached on the night of His birth were the shepherds. The wise men may have arrived about two years after His birth, not on the night of His birth. But the only people who shared with St. Mary, St. Joseph the carpenter, and Salome in the celebration of the birth of our Lord Jesus Christ were the shepherds, because the Lord Jesus Christ came to shepherd us. As we read in the Gospel of St. Luke:

> Now there were in the same country shepherds living out in the fields, keeping watch over their flock by night. And behold, an angel of the Lord stood before them, and the glory of the Lord shone around them, and they were greatly afraid. Then the angel said to them, "Do not be afraid, for behold, I bring you good tidings of great joy which will be to all people. For there is born to you this day in the

---

109 Genesis 22:17.
110 Psalms 23:1.

city of David a Savior, who is Christ the Lord. And this will be the sign to you: You will find a Babe wrapped in swaddling cloths, lying in a manger." And suddenly there was with the angel a multitude of the heavenly host praising God and saying: "Glory to God in the highest, and on earth peace, goodwill toward men!"[111]

These shepherds were vigilant, which is why they saw the angels: "There were in the same country shepherds living out in the fields, keeping watch over their flock by night." They were faithful shepherds. They did not sleep but were watching. Therefore, to whom will God reveal Himself? The glad tidings of salvation, the glad tidings of Nativity, will be revealed to the watchful and faithful people, like the shepherds who were vigilant, watchful, faithful people taking care of their flock. In the same way, if we are watchful and faithful, then God will reveal Himself to us.

4. He is the Bread of Life

Why was the Lord born in Bethlehem?

The word "Bethlehem" means "house of bread." And Jesus is the Bread of Life, as He said in the Gospel of St. John, "I am the living bread which came down from heaven."[112] Therefore, since He is the Bread of Life who came down from heaven, He chose to be

111 Luke 2:8–14.
112 John 6:51.

born in Bethlehem. And He was placed in a manger. The place itself is not called a manger, but is called a stable. The manger is like a trough in which they put the food for the animals, and because it contained hay, St. Mary put Him in it to keep Him warm. But this also has a beautiful meaning because the word "manger" in Arabic comes from the word "food," and in English from the word "to eat." Jesus is our food, our bread, as He said, "He who feeds on Me will live because of Me."[113] So now we can see that He came as a sacrifice. He offered Himself up on the cross, and by offering Himself up on the cross, then this flesh and this blood that was shed on the cross, He gave us to eat and to drink. This is why He was also born in the manger because He is the Bread of our life.

5. He is the Light of the World

In the Gospel of St. Luke, when Simeon the elder carried the Lord Jesus Christ, he said, "Lord, now You are letting Your servant depart in peace, according to Your word; for my eyes have seen Your salvation which You have prepared before the face of all peoples, a light to bring revelation to the Gentiles, and the glory of Your people Israel."[114] Jesus is the Light; He is the Sun. So He came to bring revelation to the Gentiles. The world was divided into Jews and Gentiles before the birth of our Lord Jesus Christ. The Jews were not

---

113 John 6:57.
114 Luke 2:29–32.

living in darkness, but we can say that they were living in dim light, not bright light. St. Peter said this, "And so we have the prophetic word confirmed, which you do well to heed as a light that shines in a dark place, until the day dawns and the morning star rises in your hearts."[115] He is saying that the prophets in the Old Testament were light shining in a dark place, until the day dawns and the morning star rises in your hearts. The prophetic word was like a dim light.

This resembles the electricity-generated light that we use. When the light of the sun comes, there is no longer use for this light. There is no comparison between this light and the light of the sun. St. Peter is saying that the prophetic word was like light shining in a dark place, and the Jews were the ones who had the prophecies. The Gentiles did not have prophecies or prophets. And this light guided them till the day dawned. The day dawned with the birth of Christ, and the morning star rose in your heart. Who is the morning star? It is our Lord Jesus Christ; He is the light who came into the world.

And what about the Gentiles? The Gospel of St. Matthew says, "That it might be fulfilled which was spoken by Isaiah the prophet, saying: 'The land of Zebulun and the land of Naphtali, by the way of the sea, beyond the Jordan, Galilee of the Gentiles: the people who sat in darkness have seen a great light, and upon those who sat in the region and shadow

---

115 2 Peter 1:19.

of death light has dawned.'"[116] The Gentiles are the people who sat in darkness. The Jews were living in dim light, but the Gentiles were living in complete darkness. We hear it every day in the Divine Liturgy, in the passage "Holy, Holy, Holy," "And in the last days You manifested Yourself to us, who were sitting in darkness and the shadow of death." That is why Simeon the priest, in his prophecy, said, "A light to bring revelation to the Gentiles, and the glory of Your people Israel."[117] This is because the Jews already had light, but we did not have light. "And the glory of Your people Israel"—this is because Israel obtained glory that Jesus was born as a Jewish Man from the tribe of Judah. So Jesus came as the glory of Israel and as the light to the Gentiles.

And that is why the Church, as we have said, chose the Pagan feast of the sun to be replaced by the birth of our Lord Jesus Christ. As we read also in the Gospel of St. John, "That was the true Light which gives light to every man coming into the world."[118] Jesus came as the true Light to enlighten us by His knowledge. Those who knew Him, those who believed in Him, moved from darkness to light. But those who denied Him and did not accept Him still live in darkness. The same understanding Zacharias, the father of St. John the Baptist, said in his prophecy:

---

116 Matthew 4:14–16.
117 Luke 2:29–32.
118 John 1:9.

> And you, child, will be called the prophet of the Highest; for you will go before the face of the Lord to prepare His ways, to give knowledge of salvation to His people by the remission of their sins, through the tender mercy of our God, with which the Dayspring from on high has visited us; to give light to those who sit in darkness and the shadow of death, to guide our feet into the way of peace.[119]

By "the Dayspring" is meant that as though light came as a spring, as a fountain, spreading all over the world. He shone upon all the world, to do what? "To give light to those who sit in darkness and the shadow of death, to guide our feet into the way of peace."

We as believers should be walking in the light, not in darkness. But unfortunately, some believers, although the light is there, live in darkness. There are two types of darkness. One type of darkness is when my eyes are good, but there is external darkness. The second type of darkness is when the sun is shining, but I am blind. In the Old Testament, it was the first type. Jesus had not been born, which is why we lived in darkness and the shadow of death. By the birth of Jesus, now the Sun of righteousness is shining. Those who are living in darkness are living in darkness because they are blind, not because of the absence of light. As we read in the Gospel of St. John, "That was the true Light which gives light to every man coming

119 Luke 1:76–79.

into the world."[120] Therefore, every man, not only a certain group, can be enlightened by our Lord Jesus Christ.

But who are those not enlightened, who are still in darkness? The first group is the non-believers because they rejected the Light of the world, so they still live in darkness and the shadow of death. The second group is the believers who are blinded by their sins because sin blinds the person, clouding their eyes. Although the sun is shining, I cannot see because I am blinded by my sins. Jesus came to give us light. But if I have an unrepentant heart, if I am persisting in sin, then I will not enjoy His light and will continue to live in darkness.

In the New Testament, St. Paul, before his conversion, rejected the faith in our Lord Jesus Christ, and he was persecuting the Christian believers. Although he thought that he was righteous and a Pharisee, he was in darkness. That is why when he met the Lord Jesus Christ, he lost his vision; he became blind. What is the significance of his becoming blind? The Lord wanted to tell him, "I am the Light. If you do not believe in Me, you will be blind." And St. Paul continued to be blind until Ananias laid his hands on him, and scales fell from his eyes and he was able to see again, and he was baptized. Therefore, St. Paul was an example of a person living in darkness because of his unbelief.

---

120 John 1:9.

Another example is a person who is an angel, meaning a leader of a church, but he was a sinner. In the Book of Revelation, the Scripture says, "And to the angel of the church of the Laodiceans write, 'These things says the Amen, the Faithful and True Witness, the Beginning of the creation of God.'"[121] He is sending this message to the angel of the church, to the bishop of the church, or the whole church. He said to him:

> I know your works, that you are neither cold nor hot. I could wish you were cold or hot. So then, because you are lukewarm, and neither cold nor hot, I will vomit you out of My mouth. Because you say, I am rich, have become wealthy, and have need of nothing'— and do not know that you are wretched, miserable, poor, blind, and naked.[122]

They are believers, but are also blind, still living in darkness and the shadow of death. This is why He said to him, "I counsel you to buy from Me gold refined in the fire, that you may be rich; and white garments, that you may be clothed, that the shame of your nakedness may not be revealed; and anoint your eyes with eye salve, that you may see."[123] What is the eye salve? The commandments of God, because they

---

121 Revelation 3:14.
122 Revelation 3:15–17.
123 Revelation 3:18.

are light: "Your word is a lamp to my feet and a light to my path."[124] By walking in the commandments of God, living according to the commandments of God, repenting, and seeing everything through the eyes of God, through the eyes of His commandments, this will transfer us from darkness to light.

Now then I pray you accept His Conception, and leap before Him; if not like John from the womb, yet like David, because of the resting of the Ark. Revere the enrollment on account of which you were written in heaven, and adore the Birth by which you were loosed from the chains of your birth, and honor little Bethlehem, which has led you back to Paradise.

St. Gregory of Nazianzus

Oration XXXVIII XVII. (NPNF² 7)

---

124 Psalms 119:105.

6

Symbols of the Nativity
in the Church

1. The Censer

The Church uses many symbols in the liturgy that confirm to us the truth and inevitability of the incarnation. We find, for example, that the priest puts charcoal burning with fire when he uses the censer. This charcoal burning with fire is a symbol of the incarnation, a symbol of the union of the two natures, the divinity with the humanity. The incense smoke rising from the censer and the fragrant smell of this incense remind us of the fragrance of Christ.

The censer is a symbol of the womb of the Virgin, as we say in the hymn The Golden Censer: "The golden censer is the Virgin, her aroma is our Savior." Every time we see the censer, and see the incense smoke rising from it, and see the charcoal united with the fire—this is the understanding of the incarnation; this is the understanding of the appearance of God to Moses. We are reminded of God "who offered Himself as an acceptable sacrifice upon the cross,"[125] as a sacrifice of love, so that "His good Father smelled Him in the evening on Golgotha,"[126] a sweet-smelling aroma rising before God. The Church presents to us the censer in every liturgy to speak to us about the truth of the incarnation.

God was incarnate to redeem man. God was incarnate to give us the right to become children of God. God was incarnate because He loved us—loved us to the end.[127] From this standpoint, the Church, in her fasts and practices and rites, confirms the truth of the incarnation.

2. The Divine Liturgy

The Lord Christ, in His Body and Blood, is with us in the Divine Liturgy. For so we say in the Fraction Prayer, "Behold, Immanuel our God, the Lamb of God who takes away the sin of the whole world, is with us today on this table." The presence of the Lord Jesus Christ with us, in His Body and Blood, on the altar confirms the truth of the incarnation. Was God able to give us His Body and Blood without becoming incarnate?

---

125 The Morning/Evening Offering of Incense: the priest's inaudible prayer during the procession of incense.

126 Ibid.

127 See John 13:1.

Impossible. Therefore, through the incarnation, He gave us the ability to see Him and eat of His Body and drink of His Blood, so that we may unite with Him.

In this way, when Isaiah the prophet said, "'Behold, the virgin shall be with child, and bear a Son, and they shall call His name Immanuel,' which is translated, 'God with us,'"[128] then "Immanuel, God with us" is a truth the Church has lived to present-day, two thousand years after the birth of Christ. For if this "God with us" means that God is with us, not with the Body and Blood, then one might say that God was already with His people in the Old Testament. In the New Testament, we say, "God with us, Immanuel." How? God with us, with His Body and Blood. When we eat His Body and drink His Blood, we are united with Him. Immanuel becomes God with us. God's promise before the ascension is true: "And lo, I am with you always, even to the end of the age."[129]

For truly, Immanuel is with us every day on the altar. We chant in the hymn "The Bread of Life," saying, "Around You stand the cherubim and the seraphim, and they cannot look at You. We behold You upon the altar." The seraphim, as Isaiah the prophet saw them, cover their faces because of the greatness of His invisible and ineffable glory. He said, "Above it stood seraphim; each one had six wings: with two he covered his face,"[130] while we see Him every day on

128 Matthew 1:23. See also Isaiah 7:14.
129 Matthew 28:20.
130 Isaiah 6:2.

the altar. Then Immanuel, God is with us: "Behold, Immanuel our God ... is with us today on this table."

As we have said that Christ came to redeem humanity, so He came as a lamb: "Behold! The Lamb of God who takes away the sin of the world!"[131] For this reason, we call the place where we make the Corban, that is, the bread for the Liturgy, Bethlehem, the place where Christ was born. And we call the part of the Liturgy when we come to offer the Corban, "The Offering of the Lamb." And this explains to us why Christ was born in a manger for cattle. It was not only to teach us humility, but there was a prophetic meaning also. For Christ could have been born in any other thing that is humble and simple, for the sake of teaching us humility.

But why was He born in a manger for cattle? He was born in the midst of cows, sheep, and lambs, because He is the Lamb, because He came as a sacrifice. They used to go to a sort of stable to take the sacrifices for offering. They would take a cow, a lamb, or a sheep, and offer them as a sacrifice. The Lord Christ was born in a place with sheep and cows to say that He came to the world as a lamb carrying the sin of the world and redeeming us. He was born in a manger. A manger is a trough where the fodder for the animals is placed, from which they eat. The word "manger" comes from the word "food." When the Virgin St. Mary gave birth to Christ, she put Him in the manger as a sign that

---

131 John 1:29.

He is the Bread of life. He is the Lamb and the Bread of our life. And this is accomplished in the Divine Liturgy. We say, "The Lamb," and we look at Him and see Bread. For He is a Lamb and Bread: a Lamb, carrying the sin of the world, and Bread, giving life to the world; a Lamb who dies for the world, and Bread to raise us from the death of sin.

To explain further the matter of the incarnation, in the Divine Liturgy, when the priest reaches the phrase "[He] was incarnate and became man, and taught us the ways of salvation," he places some incense into the censer which a deacon presents to him. The censer is a symbol of the womb of the Virgin, as we have said, and the incense is a symbol of Christ. As we say in the hymn "The Golden Censer," "The golden censer is the Virgin, her aroma is our Savior." The priest, in placing incense into the censer, describes the process of incarnation: God the Word descended into the womb of the Virgin. For this reason, the priest places incense into the censer as he says, "[He] was incarnate and became man." He is giving us a sort of illustration—a lesson before our eyes—of how the incarnation took place: God descended and dwelt in the womb of the Virgin and became Man.

3. The Architecture of the Church

Even in her buildings, the Church speaks about the incarnation. When the Lord Christ was born of the Virgin, He did not loosen her virginity. That is, He entered the womb of the Virgin and came out of the womb of the Virgin, and she remained a virgin, as we say in the Fraction for the Nativity, "She, being a virgin, gave birth to Him, and her virginity is sealed." There is a prophecy for this in the Old Testament when Ezekiel the prophet saw a gate that was shut in the east. The Lord entered it and came out, and it remained shut as before.[132] Therefore, in the rites of the Church, we never make a door in the church toward the east. The church has only three doors: toward the west, north, and south. This is a symbol of the birth of Christ from the Virgin without loosening her virginity. "And her virginity is sealed," as we say. Even through the architecture of the church, the Church speaks to us about the incarnation and the birth of the Lord Christ.

4. Symbols of the Incarnation in Our Prayers

Also, in our prayers, the Church speaks to us about the birth of Christ and His incarnation. Therefore, the Church arranged the Morning Prayer to remind us of the birth of Christ as well as His resurrection. Why are we reminded of the birth of Christ in the Morning Hour? Because it is said that Christ was born of the Virgin very early in the morning, fulfilling the prophecy that says, "From the womb, before the morning star I have begotten You."[133] Christ, then, was born from the womb of the Virgin very early before the morning star.

---

132 See Ezekiel 44:1–3.
133 Psalms 109:4 according to the Coptic text.

And this is the reason why the Liturgy of the Feast of Nativity finishes after midnight, because Christ was born early. Therefore, every time we pray the Morning Prayer, we remember the incarnation of the Lord Christ.

We pray some psalms that remind us of the incarnation. For example, we pray, saying, "The LORD has said to Me, 'You are My Son, today I have begotten You.'"[134] This is the psalm which we read in the Liturgy of the Feast of the Nativity. He said, "You are My Son," because He is the Son of God the Father by nature from everlasting. The word "today" means "in the fullness of time." And "I have begotten You" means "He became man."

Christ, then, has two births, according to St. Augustine:[135] a birth from God the Father from everlasting, as we say in the Creed, "Begotten of the Father before all ages.... Begotten, not created"; and the second birth is when He was born in the fullness of time from the Virgin St. Mary. The gospel of the Morning Prayer speaks about these two births. It says, "In the beginning was the Word, and the Word was with God, and the Word was God. He was in the beginning with God."[136] Then the Word was born from everlasting, and from everlasting He was with God, and He was God. The Word, who is from everlasting with God, "became flesh and dwelt among us."[137]

---

134 Psalms 2:7.
135 See St. Augustine, *Sermon XC* 2. (NPNF[1] 6).
136 John 1:1–2.
137 John 1:14.

The Word was incarnate in the fullness of time and became Man and dwelt among us. Every time we read the gospel of the Morning Prayer, we find it speaking about the two births.

5. Symbols of the Incarnation in the Holy Psalmody

The incarnation is a mystery of the Church: "And without controversy great is the mystery of godliness: God was manifested in the flesh."[138] Therefore, to explain the mystery of the incarnation and to illustrate to us the inevitability of the incarnation, why it was necessary for Christ to be incarnate, the Church put in place the Theotokias. The word "Theotokia" comes from the word "Theotokos," that is, the Mother of God. Each day there is a different Theotokia, seven Theotokias in total. And every Theotokia explains the incarnation: how God was incarnate of the Virgin Mary. Their words are very powerful.

In the Thursday Theorokia, we say, "He did not cease to be divine; He came and became the Son of Man," meaning that God, in His incarnation, in becoming the Son of Man, this did not prevent Him from still being God. He is the Son of Man and the Son of God at the same time: "He did not cease to be divine; He came and became the Son of Man, for He is the true God, who came and saved us."

---

138   1 Timothy 3:16.

The Friday Theotokia explains why Christ was incarnate and why the incarnation was an inevitable necessity. This is derived from the thought of St. Athanasius the Apostolic. It says, "He took what is ours, and gave us what is His; we praise and glorify Him, and exalt Him." "He took what is ours," that is, He took our human nature and became Man. "Gave us what is His," that is, He made us partakers of the Divine Nature. Adam desired to become like God. And why did Adam and Eve eat of the fruit of the tree of the knowledge of good and evil? To become like God. Adam wanted to be like God through pride, to exalt himself. The Lord said to him, "Adam, I want you to be like me, but not in this way. For you to be like Me, I will come down and unite with your nature, taking what is yours and giving you what is Mine. I will exalt you with Me." This is what St. Athanasius said, "But this He did, and so it was, in order that Himself taking what was ours and offering it as a sacrifice, He might do away with it, and conversely might invest us with what was His."[139] When He became the Son of Man, He made us children of God. He made us "partakers of the divine nature."[140]

In the Monday Theotokia, we say, "He shone in the flesh, taken from the Virgin, without the seed of man." We are speaking about the miracle of the incarnation: How Christ was incarnate and was born from the Virgin, without the Virgin being married, and He took a true body from her. And because He

---

139   St. Athanasius the Apostolic, *Letter LIX* 6. (NPNF[2] 4).

140   2 Peter 1:4.

is the Sun of righteousness, we say, "He shone in the flesh, taken from the Virgin."

We also describe the process of the union of divinity with humanity, and say that the Virgin was like a workplace, in the Wednesday Theotokia, "Hail to the workplace of the unparted union of the natures." That is, the two natures, the divinity and the humanity, were united together, "without mingling, without confusion, and without alteration,"[141] in the womb of the Virgin; therefore, the Virgin became the workplace of the union of the natures.

To confirm the truth of the humanity of Christ, we say to the Virgin in the Thursday Theotokia, "She gave all the form of humanity, completely, to God, the Creator and the Word of the Father." All humanity, completely, she gave to God the Creator; therefore, He became a perfect Man, and He is a perfect God.

> *"'Behold the Virgin shall conceive and bear a son, and they shall call His name Emmanuel, which is being interpreted God with us.' But what does that mean, if not that God has come in the Flesh? ... In worshipping the Lord in the flesh we do not worship a creature, but, as we said above, the Creator Who has put on the created body."*

St. Athanasius the Apostolic

Letter LX 6. (NPNF[2] 4)

---

141 The Divine Liturgy – the Confession.

7

Isaiah's Seven Effects

of the Nativity

As we reflect on the birth of Christ, we are reminded of a prophecy that Isaiah the prophet proclaimed:

> There shall come forth a Rod from the stem of Jesse, and a Branch shall grow out of his roots. The Spirit of the LORD shall rest upon Him, the Spirit of wisdom and understanding, the Spirit of counsel and might, the Spirit of knowledge and of the fear of the LORD.[142]

The rest of this chapter continues to speak about the Messiah, who is our Lord Jesus Christ. The following chapter begins by saying, "And in that day

---

142 Isaiah 11:1–2.

you will say."[143] Which day is that? It is the day of the incarnation, the day of the Nativity. I would like to say that the day of the Nativity was not a 24-hour day. We are still living the day of the incarnation till today, till the Second Coming, because the incarnation of Christ was the beginning of a new era. Therefore, when he says, "And in that day you will say," he means the new day that began with the birth of our Lord Jesus Christ. The Fathers, who interpreted the Scriptures, called the twelfth chapter, "the praise of the salvation," the song of the salvation. People rejoice in the Nativity of Christ and sing of His Nativity and salvation. In this praise, we find seven effects of the Nativity of Christ; that is, the Nativity of Christ produced seven effects in the life of humanity that are mentioned in this chapter.

1. God's Anger was Turned Away

Isaiah the prophet says, "And in that day you will say: 'O LORD, I will praise You; though You were angry with me, Your anger is turned away, and You comfort me.'"[144] The first thing the Nativity of Christ and His incarnation produced is that God's anger toward us was turned away. The anger of God began from the day of the fall of Adam and Eve when they were expelled from Paradise, from the garden of Eden. And enmity began between God and humanity. For this reason, those who died in the Old Testament went to Hades,

---

143 Isaiah 12:1.
144 Isaiah 12:1.

waiting for this day, the day of salvation, the day of the incarnation. On this day of salvation, God turned His anger away from humanity and filled our hearts with comfort and joy because God reconciled us to Himself.

Our Lord was incarnate and became Man to reconcile us to Himself. He took our punishment and fulfilled it on the cross. Therefore, when we celebrate the incarnation of the Lord Jesus Christ, we say, "O LORD, I will praise You; though You were angry with me, Your anger is turned away, and You comfort me." Unfortunately, although this time is the time of the turning away of anger, the time of comfort, the time of love as we read in Ezekiel the prophet—"When I passed by you again and looked upon you, indeed your time was the time of love"[145]—, nevertheless some of us refuse to receive God's comfort, refusing to receive the forgiveness that God gives us, refusing the salvation of God. For this reason, we do not enjoy the turning away of anger and do not enjoy comfort. Are we the type who do not accept God's salvation because we are rebellious against God, or are we the type who accept God's salvation, who are joyful and comforted because His anger is turned away from us?

2. Salvation

Not only was God's anger turned away from us, but He also saved us: "Behold, God is my salvation, I will trust

---

145 Ezekiel 16:8.

and not be afraid."[146] God, in His love for us, did not only turn away His anger from us, but also, as we say, "[He] restored Adam once more to his dominion."[147] In fact, He restored us to a higher rank than the one we were in. After the fall, we lost a particular rank in Paradise, but after the salvation, we were not restored to this rank but to a higher rank. We now unite with our Lord Jesus Christ in the Eucharist, with His Body and Blood. And St. John says, "It has not yet been revealed what we shall be, but we know that when He is revealed, we shall be like Him, for we shall see Him as He is."[148] It is a mystery what we will be in eternity. St. Peter says, "Partakers of the divine nature."[149] What does this mean? A mystery.

This is the salvation that the Lord granted me. He granted me freedom; salvation means freedom. I am no longer a servant of the devil; I am no longer a servant of sin; I am no longer a servant of death. The Lord freed me. We do not fear death because our teacher St. Paul the Apostle says, "For I am hard-pressed between the two, having a desire to depart and be with Christ, which is far better."[150] We do not fear sin because He who is with us is stronger than the one who is against us. We do not fear the devil

---

146 Isaiah 12:2.

147 The Morning/Evening Offering of Incense – The Procession of the Incense. Also see Sunday Theotokia Part 15.

148 1 John 3:2.

149 2 Peter 1:4.

150 Philippians 1:23.

because "the weapons of our warfare are not carnal but mighty in God for pulling down strongholds."[151] This is the meaning of salvation, of freedom, of having received the inheritance of the kingdom of heaven, and not only that God is no longer upset with me. He made me a child, an heir with Christ in the kingdom of heaven, as we read in the epistle to the Romans, "We are children of God, and if children, then heirs— heirs of God and joint heirs with Christ."[152] This is salvation. For this reason, when Simeon the elder took Baby Jesus in his arms after forty days of His birth, he said, "Lord, now You are letting Your servant depart in peace, according to Your word; for my eyes have seen Your salvation which You have prepared before the face of all peoples."[153]

3. Strength

Isaiah the prophet continues, saying, "For YAH, the LORD, is my strength and song; He also has become my salvation."[154] Here he is saying that the Lord— Jehovah—is my strength, the secret of my strength. God's children are not weak, but the secret of their strength is their God. During Holy Week, we chant, saying, "The Lord is my strength, and my praise, He has become to me a sacred salvation," which is taken

---

151 2 Corinthians 10:4.

152 Romans 8:17.

153 Luke 2:29.

154 Isaiah 12:2.

from the twelfth chapter of Isaiah, "For YAH, the LORD, is my strength and song; He also has become my salvation."[155] This strength benefits me in the service, in preaching in the name of Christ. This strength benefits me in bearing witness before others, bearing witness to my Lord Jesus Christ. For this reason, the Lord Jesus Christ said to the disciples, "Tarry in the city of Jerusalem until you are endued with power from on high."[156]

In the Old Testament, in the Book of Joshua, the First Book of Samuel, and the books of Kings, when an army is victorious over another army, they used to kill the king of the other army. Once they kill the king, fear would fall upon all his soldiers, and the whole army would be defeated. Our King, however, "He who keeps Israel shall neither slumber nor sleep."[157] Our King is immortal, as we say in the hymn "Holy," "Holy God, Holy Mighty, Holy Immortal." This is the strength our Lord strengthened us with. "For God has not given us a spirit of fear, but of power and of love and of a sound mind."[158] This is the spirit with which St. Peter and the disciples stood and said, "We ought to obey God rather than men."[159] This is the strength with which St. Paul stood before Nero, when St. Paul's disciples had left him, and said, "At my first defense

---

155 Isaiah 12:2.
156 Luke 24:49.
157 Psalms 121:4.
158 2 Timothy 1:7.
159 Acts 5:29.

no one stood with me, but all forsook me. May it not be charged against them."[160] This Nero was likened to a lion, but St. Paul says, "But the Lord stood with me and strengthened me…. Also I was delivered out of the mouth of the lion."[161] The children of God are strong; they do not fear, but stand and bear witness to their God mightily.

4. Security and Confidence

Security and confidence are the fourth effect that the incarnation produced. Isaiah the prophet says, "Behold, God is my salvation, I will trust and not be afraid."[162] A person is reassured, having an inner sense of security. I feel secure because I know that God loves me. I feel secure because I know that God has saved me, and He is not angry with me, and He is my strength. This made David the prophet speak in the spirit of prophecy about the day of salvation and the day of incarnation, and he said, "Yea, though I walk through the valley of the shadow of death, I will fear no evil; for You are with me,"[163] and he said, "Though an army may encamp against me, my heart shall not fear; though war may rise against me, in this I will be confident,"[164] and he also said, "God is our

---

160 2 Timothy 4:16.

161 2 Timothy 4:17.

162 Isaiah 12:2.

163 Psalms 23:4.

164 Psalms 27:3.

refuge and strength, a very present help in trouble. Therefore we will not fear, even though the earth be removed, and though the mountains be carried into the midst of the sea."[165] We will not fear because our God, He who keeps Israel, is a mighty God. This reassures a person, not only about their life on earth but also about their eternity. Would you like a greater promise from God than this? He says, "Do not fear, little flock, for it is your Father's good pleasure to give you the kingdom."[166] This thing makes God's heart rejoice, that He gives you the kingdom. Do not fear. Only the person who refuses to take this gift from God will not enter the kingdom. But the children of God, He reassures them and says, "Do not fear, little flock, for it is your Father's good pleasure to give you the kingdom."[167]

5. Joy

The birth of Christ brought joy, not only to all humankind, but also in heaven and on earth. The angels are rejoicing, and the earth is sharing in singing praises with the angels. Therefore, Isaiah the prophet says, "Therefore with joy you will draw water from the wells of salvation."[168] What are the wells of salvation? And what is the water we drink with joy from the

---

165 Psalms 46:1–2.
166 Luke 12:32.
167 Ibid.
168 Isaiah 12:3.

wells of salvation? "The wells of salvation" means the channels through which we receive salvation. Salvation that comes from God to us passes through channels, which we call the Mysteries of the Church. These are the means of grace. Therefore, the grace of the Holy Spirit and the wells of salvation pass through these channels. So they became wells of salvation for me.

What does it mean that they become wells of salvation for me? I was born in Original Sin. What do I do? I am baptized, and so I am saved from the Original Sin; here is a well of salvation. I was born as a corrupt creation. What do I do? I am anointed with Holy Myron, and so, when the Holy Spirit dwells in me, He renews my nature and makes my members members of Christ. Afterwards, when I fall into sin, what do I do? There is another well, called the Mystery of Repentance and Confession: "Wash me, and I shall be whiter than snow."[169] Also, how about the sentence of death, which is the consequence of sin? There is a well called Communion: "Whoever eats My flesh and drinks My blood has eternal life, and I will raise him up at the last day."[170]

For this reason, with the incarnation of Christ, the Mysteries of the Church have become wells of salvation for us. I come and receive of these wells with joy: I receive forgiveness of my Original Sin with joy; I receive the indwelling of the Holy Spirit in me

---

169 Psalms 51:7.
170 John 6:54.

with joy; I receive forgiveness of my sins with joy; I receive Communion and union with Christ with joy. "Our mouth is filled with gladness and our tongue with rejoicing."[171] This is what Isaiah the prophet meant when he said, "Therefore with joy you will draw water from the wells of salvation."[172] "Water" means "renewed." That is to say, there will never come a day when He says, "There is no forgiveness of sins anymore; there is no Blood of Christ anymore." So long as there is an altar, and the Body and Blood of Christ are on the altar, then there is forgiveness of sins every day, and there is resurrection from the death of sin every day. "Therefore with joy you will draw water from the wells of salvation."[173]

6. Praise and Thanksgiving

To all the aforementioned, a person's reaction will be one of praise and thanksgiving. For this reason, Isaiah says, "Praise the LORD, call upon His name; declare His deeds among the peoples, make mention that His name is exalted. Sing to the LORD, for He has done excellent things; this is known in all the earth. Cry out and shout, O inhabitant of Zion, for great is the Holy One of Israel in your midst!"[174] We find that praise is always

---

171 Prayer of Thanksgiving said by the priest after distributing the Holy Mysteries.

172 Isaiah 12:3.

173 Ibid.

174 Isaiah 12:4–6.

the language of the Church. We say that we are going to pray Midnight Praises, which means that we praise our Lord and give thanks to Him and glorify Him. Praise Him and glorify Him and exalt Him, "for He has done excellent things; this is known in all the earth."

During Communion, we drink from the well of salvation. And the deacons chant, saying, "Praise God in all His saints. Praise Him in the firmament of His power."[175] All the hymns for the Distribution are hymns of praise to the Lord. Some people who do not understand this depth begin chanting spiritual songs that have nothing to do with praising God whatsoever, and they lose the beauty of praise that goes along with the joy of drinking from the wells of salvation. Rather, the Church that has tasted salvation, her language is the language of praise. For this reason, we praise God in every Divine Liturgy, saying, "Holy, holy, holy, Lord of hosts, heaven and earth are full of Your holy glory."

7. Declaring the Lord's Name

Not only do we praise God and give thanks to Him, but we also declare His name, as Isaiah says, "Declare His deeds among the peoples, make mention that His name is exalted,"[176] and, "For He has done great things: declare this in all the earth."[177] The person who has tasted the sweetness of God cannot help but declare

---

175 Psalm 150, chanted during the distribution.

176 Isaiah 12:4.

177 Isaiah 12:5 LXX.

God's name and cry out to people and say to them, "Oh, taste and see that the LORD is good."[178] Come and see our God, how beautiful He is, how loving, how forgiving! "Declare His deeds among the peoples." The children of God, who are filled with the Spirit of God and are joyful in Him, must declare and speak of the deeds of God among the peoples, and must remind all people and creation that His name is exalted. We have a role these days, in which atheism is spreading, and people are denying and renouncing God. We have a role to call on His name and to declare His deeds among the peoples. We make mention that His name is exalted, and declare this in all the earth. We do our part, and he who has ears to hear let him hear. We have a role as children of God, that we declare His name, and speak of and invite all people to taste and see how good our God is, for "among the gods there is none like You, O Lord."[179]

For the same Person is Son of God, and was made, in the Incarnation, Son of Man, that, by His communion with each, He might link together by Himself what were divided by nature.

St. Gregory of Nyssa

Against Eunomius III.4. (NPNF[2] 5)

---

178 Psalms 34:8.

179 Psalms 86:8.

8

The Hymn of the Angels

1. Glory to God in the Highest

In the Feast of Nativity, the angels said a beautiful and powerful hymn: "Glory to God in the highest, and on earth peace, goodwill toward men!"[180] What is the meaning of "glory to God in the highest"? How did the birth of Christ cause glory to God the Father in the highest? The truth is that when the angels and all the heavenly hosts heard God promise Adam and Eve, saying to them that the woman's Seed would crush the head of the serpent,[181] they knew that God had a plan for salvation. But what this plan for salvation was, they did not know. But they were waiting to see what this plan for salvation was. No one could guess how God would save humankind. The idea that God would take flesh and become Man, and then He would carry

---

180 Luke 2:14.
181 See Genesis 3:15.

our sins, die on the cross, rise from the dead, bind the devil and crush him, descend into Hades, and save all who were taken captive by the devil in Hades—this idea was not known at all to the angels. When did they learn of it?

The angels learned of this through the incarnation of Christ, and when Christ began to form His people and His Church. Through His incarnation, forming His Church, His redemption for His people, and His salvation, the angels began to learn this mystery, the mystery of salvation which the Lord had prepared for the salvation of humankind. St. Paul the Apostle spoke about this in his epistle to the Ephesians, saying, "That now the manifold wisdom of God might be made known by the church to the principalities and powers in the heavenly places."[182] He is saying that the principalities and powers in heaven learned of the manifold wisdom of God in the salvation of humankind by means of the Church. What does "by the Church" mean? It means by the mystery of incarnation and redemption, which was accomplished in the Church.

Earlier on St. Paul said in the same epistle that his mission was to "preach among the Gentiles the unsearchable riches of Christ,"[183] preaching the goodness of Christ and the riches of His mercy, "and to make all see what is the fellowship of the mystery, which from the beginning of the ages has been hidden

---

182 Ephesians 3:10.
183 Ephesians 3:8.

in God who created all things through Jesus Christ."[184] His mission was to make the people know and to enlighten their minds with the mystery of salvation, which was hidden, meaning that it was not declared. Some people might understand the word "hidden" to mean hidden from humankind, but is it also hidden from the angels? St. Paul the Apostle says, "That now the manifold wisdom of God might be made known by the church to the principalities and powers in the heavenly places, according to the eternal purpose which He accomplished in Christ Jesus our Lord."[185] This means that this was according to the economy of God, which He prepared before all ages. This was hidden from heaven and earth, but in whom was it revealed? He accomplished it in Christ Jesus by the incarnation.

When the angels and archangels started to see the mystery of the incarnation, that God chose to become Man to redeem and save us, praise began to spread in heaven, glory spreading, glorification of God spreading in heaven. St. John of the Revelation heard this glorification: All the heavenly hosts were glorifying and praising God. Therefore, when the angels sang "Glory to God in the highest," they were saying that the incarnation of God made them—the angels—greatly marvel at the divine economy, which surpassed the minds of the heavenly and the earthly: "Great is the mystery of godliness: God was manifested in the

184 Ephesians 3:9.
185 Ephesians 3:10–11.

flesh."[186] It is like when someone devises a foolproof plan, and you find that it does succeed; therefore, you say to him, "What a wonderful plan this is! What a tremendous work this is! How beautiful!" And so the angels began to glorify God in the highest. For the incarnation of Christ, not only did it have effects on earth, but all the heavenly hosts were also astonished at the wisdom and economy of God regarding the salvation of humankind.

For this reason, the heavenly hosts shared in the implementation of this mystery when it was declared to them, as we read in the epistle of St. Paul to the Hebrews, "Are they not all ministering spirits sent forth to minister for those who will inherit salvation?"[187] The angels serve humankind to help the Lord in this beautiful plan. It is like when someone devises a plan that you are amazed at, you find yourself volunteering to help in any way. The angels truly began glorifying God through their obedience to Him, and to serve humankind so that we may inherit salvation.

What does it mean that they serve humankind? The angels began lifting our prayers before God, as St. John of the Revelation said.[188] The angels began to intercede for us before God when we fall into sin. The angels began to guard us, surround us, and protect us from the blows of the devil. The angels began to protect us from the temptations of sin. As the Scripture

---

186 1 Timothy 3:16.
187 Hebrews 1:14.
188 See Revelation 8:3–4.

says, "The angel of the LORD encamps all around those who fear Him, and delivers them."[189] When the angels learned of the mystery of the incarnation and the mystery of salvation, they glorified God: first, through praise; second, through obedience, that they became servants of humankind, serving them so that they may inherit salvation; third, through helping humankind, lifting their prayers, interceding for them, and protecting them.

Self-Examination

Do I glorify God in my life while saying, "Glory to God in the Highest"?

The Son glorified God the Father by His obedience. "He humbled Himself and became obedient to the point of death, even the death of the cross."[190] To what extent do I obey God? To what extent do I work for God's glory? To what extent do I give glory to God in everything in my life and in every success that I achieve? In every work, as St. Peter the Apostle said, "let him do it as with the ability which God supplies, that in all things God may be glorified."[191] To what extent do I rely on God in all my works. This will give glory to God: I trust in His promises, His words, His commandments. St. Paul the Apostle says a marvelous word in his first epistle to the Corinthians, "Therefore,

---

189 Psalms 34:7.

190 Philippians 2:8.

191 1 Peter 4:11.

whether you eat or drink, or whatever you do, do all to the glory of God."[192] We need to examine our lives. Is God glorified in every work I do? When people see us, do they say, "Truly, glory be to You, Lord"? Or do people sometimes say, "Look, Christians do such-and-such"? And as the Scripture says, "Because of whom the way of truth will be blasphemed."[193] Do we really glorify our Lord or not?

2. Peace on Earth

With the incarnation and the Nativity of Christ, peace began to be on the earth. About this peace, St. Paul the Apostle spoke a beautiful word in his epistle to the Ephesians, saying, "For He Himself is our peace."[194]

Peace Between God and Man

Christ came, and peace rested upon the earth, because reconciliation was fulfilled between God and man, man and his brother, and man and himself. The first reconciliation is between God and man. When Adam and Eve fell, enmity arose between God and man. And this enmity was the most manifest in the Holy of Holies, which is where God came down upon the cover of the ark, because no one was permitted to enter except the high priest, and this only once a

192 1 Corinthians 10:31.

193 2 Peter 2:2.

194 Ephesians 2:14.

year. There was a veil that was always closed, as a sign that the gate of heaven was closed before men because of the enmity. As the Scripture says, "And He placed cherubim at the east of the garden of Eden, and a flaming sword which turned every way, to guard the way to the tree of life."[195] This is so that no one would eat from it.

Even in worship in the Old Testament, the door of the tabernacle of meeting and of Solomon's temple was toward the east, and the Holy of Holies was toward the west, because the east symbolizes the presence of God. The garden of Eden was in the east, and the sun, which illumines the world, rises from the east. For this reason, God teaches us to pray toward the east. The east reminds us of God's presence. In the Old Testament, all the worship was toward the west, looking toward the west, to remember that they were expelled, because the garden of Eden, from which man was expelled, was in the east, and so his face was toward the west, and his back toward the east. This is why, now when the priest performs the procession of incense in church, he says when looking toward the western door, "He opened the gate of Paradise and restored Adam once more to his dominion."

There was enmity between God and man. When God appeared to Moses, the people could not come near, and whoever would come near the mountain was

---

195 Genesis 3:24.

to be put to death.[196] Only Moses went up and spoke with God. Then God spoke with Moses, and Moses would tell the people. There was always a mediator between God and man. St. Paul speaks about this mediator in his epistle to the Hebrews, saying, "God, who at various times and in various ways spoke in time past to the fathers by the prophets, has in these last days spoken to us by His Son."[197] That is to say, God spoke to our fathers and forefathers in the Old Testament by the prophets, but by the incarnation of Christ, He spoke to us by His Son. Christ came to reconcile us to God the Father, and this reconciliation was fulfilled through the cross. "For through Him we both have access by one Spirit to the Father."[198] He united me with Him, and in Christ, I became a son of God the Father; and in Christ, I can stand and speak with God the Father, and say to Him, "Our Father who art in heaven."

Peace Between Man and His Brother

The second aspect of peace is that He reconciled the Jews with the Gentiles and the people with the peoples, as St. Paul said, "For He Himself is our peace, who has made both one, and has broken down the middle wall of separation."[199] Only the Jews were allowed to enter

---

196 See Exodus 19:12.

197 Hebrews 1:1–2.

198 Ephesians 2:18.

199 Ephesians 2:14.

the temple. And there was an outer court called the court of the Gentiles. In the past, the people of God were the Jews only. The world was divided into Jews and Gentiles. Everyone who was not a Jew was called a Gentile. And there was a middle wall, separating the Jews from the Gentiles. Our Lord Jesus Christ came and reconciled the Jews with the Gentiles, "uniting and reconciling the heavenly with the earthly, the people with the peoples,"[200] and has broken down the middle wall of separation. St. Mark, who was Jewish in origin, went and preached to the land of Egypt, which was Gentile. The flight of Christ into the land of Egypt was a sign of the Gentiles' acceptance. For this reason, the Church arranged that the readings of the first Sunday after the Feast of Nativity speak to us about the acceptance of the Gentiles, reconciliation, and the peace accomplished between the people and the peoples, between the Jews and the Gentiles, between man and his brother.

Peace Between Man and Himself

The third aspect of peace speaks about how God reconciled man with himself. Before this, when a person fell into sin, if he had no knowledge through the eye of faith that God had promised this salvation, he would fall into despair and would suffer from depression, fear, and anxiety. But the Lord came to take away these from my heart: to take away my fear, to take away the feeling of guilt from me, to take away

---

200 The Syrian Fraction.

shame and disgrace from me. And He came to give man peace, peace that does not depend on the external circumstances, but rather peace that springs from within the person. He gave us His Holy Spirit, and we read in the epistle to the Galatians that "the fruit of the Spirit is love, joy, peace..."[201] And He says, "Peace I leave with you, My peace I give to you; not as the world gives do I give to you,"[202] inner peace, "the peace of God, which surpasses all understanding, will guard your hearts and minds through Christ Jesus."[203] "On earth peace"[204]—Christ came, and so He made peace between man and God, between man and his brother, and between man and himself.

Self-Examination

Am I a peacemaker?

How many people am I angry with? How many people do I not want to be reconciled with? How many people do I not greet when I see them? And then do we say, "Peace on earth"? To how many do I cause problems, upsetting people with each other? Do I slander people? Do I cause problems and fights with my family at home? There is a demon called the demon of Feasts. Many people fight on Feasts, because this demon does not like us to be glad and rejoice in the

---

201 Galatians 5:22.
202 John 14:27.
203 Philippians 4:7.
204 Luke 2:14.

Feast. Do we, I wonder, make the hymn of the angels come true, and we say, "Truly, on earth peace"? And when I see someone I am angry at, I should go to him and greet him, as Christ became incarnate to reconcile us. I break out of the prison of hatred, resentment, and fighting. I crush this prison and break out of it, so that I may make peace. This is the meaning of "on earth peace." How do we say, "on earth peace," while we are oversensitive toward each other and there are barriers between us? In the Divine Liturgy of St. Gregory, we say, "The middle wall You have broken down." Are we breaking down the walls that we have built between us and our brethren or not? Will we repent, I wonder, and be reconciled with our Lord or not? If there is peace between God and me, and between my brother and me, then I will have peace with myself.

3. Goodwill Toward Men

The incarnation of Christ proclaimed God's pleasure[205] toward man. What does "goodwill toward men" mean? It means that God's pleasure and gladness are directed toward man. God is pleased with us. How did Christ's incarnation proclaim God's pleasure in man, that He loves us and has a beautiful plan for us? First, it revealed to us that God does not desire the death of a sinner, but that he return and live.[206] What are we?

---

205 The word for "goodwill" in the Arabic verse can be translated as "pleasure" or "joy."
206 See Ezekiel 33:11.

We are but dust and ashes. Imagine how marvelous it is that God became incarnate and died and rose—all this to redeem us who are but dust and ashes! When someone has a cat or a dog and takes great care of them, we might say, "Why all this care? Why spend so much? It is only a little animal. Why is he giving it so much care?" Now imagine, we are dust to God. God created us from the dust and ashes.

But although we are dust and ashes and as nothing before Him, we are very precious to God's heart. God did not spend on us money as St. Peter the Apostle says, "You were not redeemed with corruptible things, like silver or gold,"[207] but rather, what God did for us surpasses the human mind. God becomes Man and accepts being poor while He is rich. He accepts humiliation and having nowhere to lay His head. He accepts that His creation scourges Him, spits on Him, insults and reviles Him. He accepts carrying our sins in His body and becoming a curse for our sakes. All this is so that He may save us. What is the reason for all this? God's goodwill is toward men. God loves us exceedingly and is pleased to save us. St. Paul the Apostle says, "For the joy that was set before Him [He] endured the cross, despising the shame."[208] What joy is it that was set before Him? The joy of the cross, that God may save us.

Truly, the incarnation declared to us the extent to which we are the object of God's pleasure. St. John the

---

207 1 Peter 1:18.
208 Hebrews 12:2.

beloved says, "Behold what manner of love the Father has bestowed on us, that we should be called children of God!"[209] "In this, the love of God was manifested toward us, that God has sent His only begotten Son into the world."[210] God sent His Son into the world; there is no greater love than this. If God only saved us, this would be more than we ask or understand.[211] Not only did God save us, but He also has united us with Himself—has made us one with Him. He said, "He who eats My flesh and drinks My blood abides in Me, and I in him."[212] He filled us with the Holy Spirit and made us a dwelling place for Him: "Do you not know that you are the temple of God and that the Spirit of God dwells in you?"[213] He filled us with the fruit of the Spirit, granted us of His attributes, and made us partners in the work with Him.

As we say in the Friday Theotokia, "He took what is ours, and gave us what is His; we praise and glorify Him, and exalt Him." What did the Lord take that is ours? Sin, the curse, the disgrace, the poverty—all these He took. St. Paul the Apostle says, "That though He was rich, yet for your sakes He became poor,"[214] "For He made Him who knew no sin to be sin for

---

209 1 John 3:1.

210 1 John 4:9.

211 See The Divine Liturgy of St. Gregory: passage before the Introduction to the Fraction.

212 John 6:56.

213 1 Corinthians 3:16.

214 2 Corinthians 8:9.

us,"[215] and, "Christ has redeemed us from the curse of the law, having become a curse for us."[216] And what did He give us? He gave us His glory; we became glorified with Him.[217] He gave us His inheritance; we became heirs with Him.[218] He gave us His throne, for He said, "To him who overcomes I will grant to sit with Me on My throne."[219] Why, Lord? Why all of this? He says, "Because I am pleased with you." "Do not fear, little flock, for it is your Father's good pleasure to give you the kingdom."[220] For this reason, His goodwill is toward men. We do not deserve His goodwill toward us and being pleased in us. Truly, the birth of Christ led to glorification and praise to God in the highest, brought forth peace on earth, and made us become enlightened and know how much God is pleased in us.

Self-Examination

Do I gladden God's heart?

We say, "Goodwill toward men," or "His goodwill toward men."[221] Do I, I wonder, gladden God's heart? He did all this because He loves me. There is a beautiful verse said about John the Baptist, "Many will rejoice at

---

215 2 Corinthians 5:21.

216 Galatians 3:13.

217 See Romans 8:17.

218 Ibid.

219 Revelation 3:21.

220 Luke 12:32.

221 The word "goodwill" in the Arabic verse could also mean "pleasure" or "joy."

his birth."[222] When God sees me, does He rejoice, or is He saddened? When God saw the wickedness during Noah's time, the Scripture says, "And the LORD was sorry that He had made man on the earth, and He was grieved in His heart."[223] When God sees me, my deeds, and my behavior, will there be goodness toward men, or am I a reason for sorrow and pain to God's heart because of my disobedience, my rebellion, my distancing myself from Him, my bad behavior, my revolt against His commandments? Also, am I a cause of joy to my family, my parents, my siblings, and my relatives? Am I a cause of joy to the Church servants and to the priests who are serving me? Am I a cause of joy to my coworkers and to the people whom I am serving, my superiors at work? Am I a cause of joy to those who are outside, the unbelievers? When they deal with me, do they feel joyful and at peace, or is the opposite true?

When the angels saw God's love for us, they said, "His goodwill toward men." I wonder, am I truly a cause of joy to God and His children or not? This is the Feast of Nativity: We glorify God in our lives, and should be peacemakers, and should be a cause of joy to all those around us. As we pray in the Agpeya, in the litanies of the Sixth Hour, and say, "You have filled all with joy, O Savior, when You came to help the world. Lord, glory be to You."

---

222 Luke 1:14.

223 Genesis 6:6.

Christ is born, glorify Him. Christ from heaven, go out to meet Him. Christ on earth; be exalted. Sing unto the Lord all the whole earth; and that I may join both in one word, Let the heavens rejoice, and let the earth be glad, for Him Who is of heaven and then of earth. Christ in the flesh, rejoice with trembling and with joy; with trembling because of your sins, with joy because of your hope.

St. Gregory of Nazianzus

Oration XXXVIII I. (NPNF[2] 7)

9

The Feelings We Get from Christ's Nativity

We stand in amazement before our God, who is very humble, who is very loving, who is very caring, to the extent that He made such a decision as to empty Himself, and to take the form of man and be among us. Indeed, "Great is the mystery of godliness: God was manifested in the flesh."[224]

1. The Sense of Security and Safety

The birth of Christ stirs many feelings in our hearts. The sense of security and safety is the first of these feelings. When our Lord found that there was a danger threatening the life of humankind, He did not hesitate

---

224 1 Timothy 3:16.

at all to empty Himself and take an ordinary form,[225] and be "found in appearance as a man,"[226] to save us from this danger, and to liberate us from the bondage of the devil, and to give us true and better life, in which there is freedom. As He said, "I have come that they may have life, and that they may have it more abundantly."[227] For this reason, the psalm says, "Blessed is the nation whose God is the LORD."[228] Blessed is the nation whose God is our Lord Jesus Christ. This gives us a sense of security. He emptied Himself for us, and cares for us, and looks after our needs, and examines the dangers that threaten us, and He always protects us.

2. The Feeling of True Joy

The Lord is in our midst. He is with us; Immanuel, God with us. He is not a God whom we cannot reach. Neither is He a God with whom we cannot speak. But rather, He is the God who humbled Himself and lived among us. "That which was from the beginning, which we have heard, which we have seen with our eyes, which we have looked upon, and our hands have handled, concerning the Word of life—the life was manifested."[229] How intensely do the feelings of joy overwhelm our hearts when we learn that our Lord

---

225 See Philippians 2:7.

226 Philippians 2:8.

227 John 10:10.

228 Psalms 33:12.

229 1 John 1:1–2.

took from the Virgin Mary all the form of humanity, with perfection,[230] to sanctify it and purify it. Our Lord lifted up the standing of humanity and raised our honor when He became Man like us. He became Man like us so that He may make us children of God and partakers of His Nature. Therefore, every time we stand still and contemplate the birth of our Lord Jesus Christ, the feelings of joy overwhelm our hearts, and happiness fills our lives, like the Magi when they saw the star, "they rejoiced with exceedingly great joy."[231]

3. The Feelings of Love, Acceptance, and Care

A person feels very joyful when they feel that they are loved; they are not rejected. There is someone who cares for them and accepts them as they are. God loves us. "God demonstrates His own love toward us, in that while we were still sinners, Christ died for us."[232] The devil portrays to us that if we are still struggling against sin, God does not love us or care for us. But the opposite is the truth, because God's love for us is unconditional. He loves us and cares for us while we are still sinful. He loves us and cares for us because He "did not come to call the righteous, but sinners, to repentance."[233] And as Ezekiel the prophet heard a voice, saying, "When I passed by you again and looked

---

230 See Thursday Theotokia.
231 Matthew 2:10.
232 Romans 5:8.
233 Mark 2:17.

upon you, indeed your time was the time of love."[234] Beware of believing the devil who says to you that God does not love you. God hates sin but loves the sinner. Beware of believing the devil who says to you that God will forsake you because of your sins. It is impossible that God would forsake His children and His creation. He promised us and said, "I will never leave you nor forsake you,"[235] and "I am with you always, even to the end of the age."[236] This is the love that stirs in us the feelings of repentance. This is the love that makes us desire to return to God with all our hearts.

4. The Feeling of Being Treated Equally

The birth of our Lord stirs also in us the feeling of being equal, that God came for all, that His love, His incarnation, and His salvation were granted equally to all. He did not show partiality between one nation and another, nor one group of people and another. As the angels appeared to the Jewish shepherds and announced to them the wondrous birth of Christ, so did a star—which is an angelic power—appear to the Magi who were of the Gentiles, and not of the Jews, and announced to them the birth of Christ. It is as though God were saying, "I am coming for all. I am not coming for a particular nation nor a particular group, but I am rather coming for all, for the Jews and for the Gentiles."

---

234 Ezekiel 16:8.

235 Hebrews 13:5.

236 Matthew 28:20.

Christ was born poor, as St. Paul the Apostle says, "Though He was rich, yet for your sakes He became poor."[237] He was born poor to tell us that He came for the poor and for the rich, for the sinner and for the righteous, for men and for women, for children and for elders, for slaves and for the free. He came for all because the love of God has no partiality: God's love is for all. This is equality because we are all His creation and "the work of His hands."[238]

5. The Feeling of Peace

If someone were upset with me, or if I wronged someone, especially if this someone was of great stature, and then I heard that this person was coming to me, I might be scared, thinking that this person was coming to take revenge on me, or to punish me, or to chastise me. The truth, however, is that, despite our rebellion and disobedience and sins that we directed against God, the Lord did not come to take revenge on us, or to punish us, or to chastise us, but rather He came to reconcile us and make peace with us. He came as the King of peace and said, "Peace I leave with you, My peace I give to you; not as the world gives do I give to you."[239] And when the two cities refused to receive Him, James and John came and said, "Lord, do You want us to command fire to come down from heaven

237 2 Corinthians 8:9.

238 Job 34:19.

239 John 14:27.

and consume them, just as Elijah did?"[240] The Lord said to them, "You do not know what manner of spirit you are of. For the Son of Man did not come to destroy men's lives but to save them."[241] God came to reconcile us to Himself, to reconcile us also to one another, and to reconcile man to himself. He came to make peace, to unite a nation with another, and man with God.

6. The Feelings of Gratitude and Thanksgiving

When we experience all these beautiful feelings—the feelings of joy, love, peace, equality, wonder at the incarnation of the Son of God—at the end, we find our hearts full of feelings of gratitude and thanksgiving. We thank God with all our hearts. Our lives are incapable of sufficiently thanking God. Even if we give every moment of our lives to God, we remain incapable of giving Him the thanks befitting His greatness and glory.

We truly thank You, Lord, with all our hearts for Your wondrous incarnation, for Your humility. We thank You because You were content to be born in our midst, because You became Man to make us children of God. We glorify You; we bless You; we praise You forever and ever. Amen.

---

240 Luke 9:54.
241 Luke 9:55–56.

✠

And this was the wonderful thing that He was at once walking as man, and as the Word was quickening all things, and as the Son was dwelling with His Father. So that not even when the Virgin bore Him did He suffer any change.

St. Athanasius the Apostolic

On the Incarnation of the Word 17.5. (NPNF^2 4)